CW00509628

VAL & I
A LOVE STORY

VAL & I
A LOVE STORY

John Salmon

Matador
Unit E2 Airfield Business Park,
Harrison Road, Market Harborough,
Leicestershire. LE16 7UL
Tel: 0116 2792299
Email: books@troubador.co.uk
Web: www.troubador.co.uk/matador
Twitter: @matadorbooks

ISBN 978 1803132 211

British Library Cataloguing in Publication Data.
A catalogue record for this book is available from the British Library.

Printed and bound in Great Britain by 4edge Limited
Typeset in 11pt Sabon MT by Troubador Publishing Ltd, Leicester, UK

Matador is an imprint of Troubador Publishing Ltd

IN LOVING MEMORY OF

Valerie Hazel Salmon
My dear wife and the love of my life

Contents

Prologue

After my dear wife, Valerie, died on the 16th of February 2019, I tried to think of a suitable memorial for her. As she had been cremated, at her request, I had no grave to visit. She loved flowers, particularly roses. I came up with two solutions.

Today, as you enter our bungalow here in Dawlish, you will find a rather empty hallway. You will see two framed photographs: one of Val, the other of the two of us. Between the photographs are two of her favourite vases; one containing a single red rose, the other, a larger one, containing a dozen roses. They are real roses and I religiously change them on a weekly basis. This simple memorial works for me. As I leave and enter by the front door, the first thing I see is Val's face in the photos and the roses.

The second memorial is this book.

The simple truth is that the love that Val gave to me changed my life completely. She filled my heart with warmth, tenderness, care and affection; all very special things. I believe that I did the same for her. In a long and very happy marriage, I never once stopped loving her. I hope that I am able to honour her memory, salute her and amply convey my feelings for her by recording some of our life together in the pages of this book. It is from my heart; it will inevitably become my eulogy to Val, but it is also our love story.

From our first kiss on the 24th of December 1955 to our last kiss on the 16th of February 2019, our love was deep, faithful, true and quite wonderful. It is not easy to choose what to include and what to leave out in attempting to cover sixty-one years of marriage. To record and describe events, travel and even anecdotes is comparatively easy and straightforward. To communicate feelings, and deep meaningful emotion, is a much more difficult task. I start this book with a strong desire to do both, and I can only hope that I am able to go some way in achieving these aims.

My hope is that this book may, in some small way, help me and others to remember Val and the love that we shared for so many years.

Chapter 1

Love at First Sight

As a nineteen-year-old young man, I considered myself to be confident, reasonably well educated and quite worldly-wise. It was 1955 and I had just embarked on a career in the Royal Air Force. I had joined 42 Squadron at RAF St Mawgan in Cornwall, a coastal command station just outside Newquay. This was particularly handy for me, as my home was in Exeter and I could still enjoy my mother's cooking at weekends!

I soon got used to spending most weekends in Exeter; these consisted of depositing my weekly laundry for my mother to do, eating everything she cooked and generally lazing around. I was stationed in a very pleasant part of the country with some beautiful beaches nearby and lovely countryside around it.

My involvement with the opposite sex was in a state of flux at this time. I had been in quite a long relationship with an older woman, Marion, but this had recently come to an end, due to me. She had been making it quite obvious that she was keen on a more permanent arrangement, possibly leading to marriage. An attitude guaranteed to put the 'frighteners' on me! She didn't give up easily and it took several weeks for her to 'get the message'. The two years or so of this affair did have, however, some positive outcomes for me. She was older, more experienced, and she did an excellent job in advancing my sex education! I was no longer a fumbling novice when it came to the fair sex; I was also no longer a virgin. I was very grateful for that and the educational aspects of our affair; I had certainly moved on from my previous few younger girlfriend adventures.

No longer having a steady girlfriend, it inevitably became easier to make new friendships in the Mess. I suppose, quite naturally, one honed in on chaps who were from your part of the world, mainly Exeter and Plymouth. The understandable affinity led to friendships that were sound and mutually advantageous. In those days, few of us could afford cars. We did manage to acquire bicycles, which saved our legs around the base. Film depictions of young RAF chaps driving around country lanes in open-top MGs were really quite far-fetched and far from reality.

Among my particular group of friends at St Mawgan were Johnny Francis, Dickie Bond and John Gaskell, all from Exeter. They were to play an important part in the start of this love story. Having dodged as many weekend RAF duties as we could, our main aim in life was to collect a weekend pass to leave the base and look forward to a trip to Exeter. We all got on well together and we had common goals in life, very simple ones! A few coffees in the mornings, a few drinks in the evenings and some female company to spice things up.

Early in this series of weekends, Johnny Francis persuaded me to join his small group of friends who met up on a Saturday morning in Exeter. We would wander around the shops, drink coffee, smoke a lot of cigarettes and generally laze around. Anyone who had a current girlfriend would relegate her time to later in the day on a Saturday. The lads came first!

The fact that we were all six foot tall, quite physically fit and reasonably well dressed, with ties and sometimes blazers, meant that we usually kept free from trouble with other local lads in pubs or at dances. The only rivals that we ever had on the young ladies front were from the occasional visits by officer cadets from Royal Marine Commando, Lympstone. No one fell out with them!

The first significant event in this story happened around this time. Some of the lads suggested one Saturday that we all go into Currys, the high street shop. Evidently, they had just opened a new record department. It would, it seemed, be possible to listen to records for an hour or so, for free! I followed the others down to the basement record department. One or two of them had already been in there and they were familiar with the surroundings, and also familiar with the two young ladies who worked there.

I was introduced to Val Brockley, the manageress, who had set up the department from scratch for Currys, and Jeanette Ford, her assistant. This was a rather special meeting! I set my eyes on – no handshakes only a 'Hi' – Valerie Hazel Brockley for the first time in my life. This young lady, who was just nineteen at the time, was to become the love of my life, my soulmate, my special one, and eventually my wife for sixty-one years!

It was Christmas 1955. I had been using all my natural talent for chatting up girls on one new and already, in my mind, special target, Valerie. I was aware that on the third finger of her left hand, there was a rather splendid piece of jewellery: an engagement ring! Val made it quite clear to me that she was engaged to be married. She was engaged to a young man in the Royal Navy called Peter Forbes, who hailed from Burnham-on-Sea in Somerset.

They had met at a dance in Plymouth. I already knew that Val loved ballroom dancing, that she was good at it and that she did some part-time teaching work at Marcina's Dance School in Exeter. Ballroom dancing was certainly not my forte, although I could perform a reasonable waltz and a passable quickstep. Val had visited her fiancé's home in Somerset, stayed there, met his parents and attended through a happy engagement party there.

The fact that she was engaged to another chap did not deter me, however, in my pursuit of Val. Cupid had already plunged the proverbial arrow into my heart. Christmas Eve, 1955, was a really momentous day in both our lives, but we did not know it then.

I did on occasion at weekends go into town with an old school friend, Glenn Luscombe, and we would often have a drink or two and end up going to the cinema. Christmas Eve, 1955, was such an occasion. I had already arranged to meet Glenn in the evening at 6.30 pm. During the afternoon, I was in my usual spot in Currys talking to Val over the counter. Merely talking is not really what I was doing; I had moved into overdrive with my chatting up of Val. Perhaps it was the fact that it was Christmas Eve, a special evening of anticipation and excitement, who knows, but I was particularly determined that Val should have a good evening out, preferably with me!

It seems that her fiancé was away at sea and she had planned to go dancing, with some girlfriends acting as chaperones for her. My chat-up line was that she could go dancing anytime, any night, but she could only go out with me on that night, as I was only on weekend leave and when would another opportunity arise? I somehow managed to use humour, charm and whatever it took to persuade her to go out that evening on a date with me. She made it quite clear that it was a 'one-off' and that there was nothing to be taken from it. Naturally, I agreed to her every word! She insisted that she would have to go home first after work and that she would meet me at seven outside the Currys shop. I can still clearly remember a feeling of walking on air as I skipped up the stairs and out of Currys early that evening.

Glenn was waiting for me at 6.30 and I had no qualms about informing him that I had to cancel our evening together. He was none too happy but departed nevertheless, leaving me outside Currys smoking the inevitable cigarette. Val turned up on time and I greeted her cautiously, that is, very politely, and I made sure I was not being too forward. I did not hold her hand as we decided to go to the pictures. She chose *Pete Kelly's Blues* at the Savoy Cinema in the high street, not far to walk, London Inn Square as it was known then. I instinctively felt that I had to be on my best behaviour with Val. She was a lady, so good manners were essential at all times. This first date was important to me. Later, I discovered that Val felt the same way herself.

We arrived at the Savoy Cinema and I bought tickets. I was careful to buy good tickets. There were many choices so I bought a middle-priced pair, downstairs, but not the cheapest. I was on my best behaviour. Even then, on that first date, there was something magical about it. I could not explain it then in 1955, or now in 2019. I was feeling something different. I had experienced some excitement on dates with girls before but nothing like this; it was very special.

I bought Val some expensive sweets and we walked, still not holding hands, to the cinema auditorium entrance. In those days, uniformed usherettes, complete with torches, met patrons at the door. We were greeted by a short, dark-haired young lady usherette who immediately broke into a welcoming smile.

"Hello, John, how are you? Lovely to see you again."

I was flabbergasted and a little dismayed, as I had already noticed Val's rather surprised and clearly unhappy reaction to the familiarity shown by the usherette.

This young lady was Margaret Turner, at the time the steady girlfriend of my long-term school friend George Hill. More critical for me, at that moment, was the fact that I had myself already dated Margaret on a few occasions, particularly as George was now in the Royal Navy and often away. Previously, Margaret and I had kissed and cuddled, I had walked her home and we got on quite well! Suffice to say that it was a rather embarrassing situation at the time.

Margaret switched on her torch and ushered us into the dark auditorium. She moved some cinemagoers along in their seats and very astutely guided Val and I into seats in the back row, the courting area! I swear that I heard Margaret chuckle to herself as she left us. It took some time before I could even look at Val in the dark cinema. Eventually, she whispered the question, "She knows you, then?"

I managed to whisper a reply, explaining that she was my friend's girlfriend and that George was in the Navy and away in Plymouth. What Val made of that at the time, I will never know. Here she was on a date with me, being engaged to a chap in the Navy, currently at sea. It must have been a hard and difficult moment for my darling Val. Margaret Turner eventually married George and they are still together and living in Plymouth. Later in our marriage, Val told me that she thought I was a 'fast worker' in the dating stakes and that she had guessed Margaret Turner and I had form together.

After some time in the cinema, I plucked up courage and took hold of Val's hand. Before the film ended, my arm had crept around her shoulder and, I felt, she responded, a bit reluctantly, by leaning against me. To be absolutely honest, there was a moment or two when I thought I've blown this, and she is not going to let me see her again. I was desperate to improve matters. We left the cinema at about 10 pm, and keen to improve my chances, I suggested that I take Val for a drink. We went around the corner from the Savoy where there was a bar called the London Inn. We walked into the lounge bar to be greeted by a couple who were already in there: Valerie Heale and Peter Jeffrey.

What a coincidence! Valerie had been a long-time friend from school of Val's and Peter Jeffrey had been at Hele's Boys' Grammar School with me. Things were certainly moving rapidly for Val and I on our first-ever date. After about half an hour of introductions, small talk and trying to get over our mutual embarrassment and nervousness, Val and I left the London Inn. We walked along New North Road, heading for St David's, towards Val's home in Tavistock Road. I gently took her hand as we slowly walked along. We talked mainly about the coincidence of meeting the other couple in the London Inn. That was remarkable, meeting old school friends, as a couple.

Looking back now, I knew that Val was special even then. This was somehow different and exceptional. I am now quite sure that this was meant to be. The Almighty had brought us together. What I did not know then was that Val had suffered in her childhood days. She had been physically abused by her father, and she had been brought up in a very unhappy home environment. But I did know then that this girl was special, very special! I felt that I was walking home a lady of some class and that I was even holding her warm little hand!

We eventually arrived at Tavistock Road and as we approached her front door, I was literally shaking inside. For a so-called 'man of the world', experienced at dating and so confident, I was suddenly a nervous wreck. What to do? How would I cope? What strategy to adopt? I just couldn't think straight; I didn't know what to do. Val stood in front of her house door and turned towards me. We were no longer holding hands. She gave me a beautiful smile and I leaned towards her. It was the softest, most gentle, tender and loving kiss, quite long in duration and really quite fabulous!

Val said goodnight, turned and was gone. One kiss, for me, that was failure, or it would have been. But no, I felt great. I almost skipped up her road. It was too late for a bus home so I had a long walk ahead of me to the other side of town. I set off in a state of great excitement; the walk was nothing. It mattered little, because on our walk home she had agreed that I could have another date with her and, to top it all, we had kissed, the first one ever!

Chapter 2

Absence Makes the Heart Grow Fonder

Our early courting days were governed by the situation I was in at the time. I was in the Royal Air Force and stationed at RAF St Mawgan, in Cornwall. This meant that my visits to Exeter, already quite regular at weekends, were to become very important. How I got through the week's duties I do not know.

I was absolutely smitten. Val filled my thoughts and I made phone calls to her nearly every day. Luckily, her parents had a telephone, quite a rare thing in 1956. It was long before the days of all homes having a telephone. Mobile phones were a dream to be found only in the pages of science fiction! In these first few weeks of 1956, I had to resort to writing letters. I poured out my heart to Valerie in pages, and looking back, I must have been good at it too. She wrote back to every letter I sent her during the weekdays, and I literally lived for the weekends so that I could see Val again. How I managed to get most weekends off I'll also never know, but I did. I was so excited on a Friday when I set off for Exeter again.

Our dates were marvellous. My parents would see very little of me. Val was working on Saturdays and I could be found propping up her counter in Currys record department; the staff there were very good to me. In retrospect, they must have been aware that we were in love. I would take Val out on a Saturday evening. We would have meals, sitting in cafés drinking coffee and holding hands. We didn't want anything other than each other; we talked and talked. I soon discovered that my darling Val had endured a terrible home life, and that made me love her even more, if that was possible!

Early in January 1956, we were inseparable at weekends. I took her to meet my parents and I met her parents. We had to do this early in our courting because, like me, Val was rarely home at weekends. It was more critical for Val because she was the only thing that kept her parents together and kept them from violent rows, separations and even fights. They had got used to having her at home to 'keep the peace'. As she was now a grown-up twenty-year-old, she could, and did, keep their marriage together. I found it particularly difficult to keep my own anger and disquiet under control when I was in her parents' presence. I gradually understood what sort of life she had endured and I vowed to take her away from it, even in those early courting days.

Val was great. She was polite and helpful with my parents. She never complained and never spoke about her troubled home life. On visits to my grandparents' bungalow, she loved to help my gran and to talk to my war-hero grandfather. They both took to Val instantly and a great bond was soon built up between them. Looking back now, I realise that Val loved the fact that she could spend time in a normal family home with love, care and decency all around. She fitted in so smoothly and it was a joy to see her happy in my family home. I, of course, adored her, and our dates continued to fill our lives.

After just three weeks of our courting, Val told me that she had broken off her engagement to Peter and that she had sent back her engagement ring and some presents that she had received. I felt great. The physical side of our courting had moved on very little. We embraced, we kissed and we held hands and that was it. There was no way I was going to jeopardise my love of Val by offending her in any way. She was a lady and I knew it.

My previous girlfriends had been rather different. I had been used to taking liberties whenever I could get away with it. Heavy petting was the norm, which included mutual sexual awareness and satisfaction. This was not the case with Val. In the first three months of our relationship, we kissed a lot and held each other closely, whenever we could. This was usually late at night, on the way to her home. Taking her home, I would deliberately use a route which gave us a wall to lean against so that we could kiss and cuddle. That was all it was and I was as happy as could be. Naturally, I got excited at times, but I kept control; no way was I going to upset Val.

She was often responsive, however, and I knew that, when the time was right, we would move on in the physical side of things. Her kisses were lovely and enough for me; holding her tiny hand and being close to her was a bonus. I can clearly remember going home after our usual Sunday together, very late at night. I would kiss her goodnight and then set off for the bus at the railway station close to her home in St David's. Then before she had arrived at her front door, I would run back to her and take her in my arms for an 'extra' kiss. She loved it – she would tell me off.

"You've missed your bus," she would say.

"Never mind, I'll walk," and I did.

The walk took up to three quarters of an hour to arrive at my home. My mother would leave me a plate of sandwiches and I am sure she understood that I was in love. I would fall asleep in my bedroom with a smile on my face.

A major change came early in 1956. Our courtship, the many weekends of bliss together, the letters and phone calls midweek, were dealt a crushing blow. I received an unexpected posting by the RAF. I was to report to No. 300 Signals Unit, a quasi-secret radar unit of Second Allied Tactical Air Force, a part of NATO and based in Germany! The unit was part of a chain of spy units monitoring the Soviet bloc in Europe. The Cold War was at its height at that time and NATO was the West's defensive shield to any possible Soviet aggression. 300 Signals Unit was then operating in Northern Germany and had its base at RAF Oldenburg, from where it kept an eye on Soviet Bloc forces in the northern part of the DDR (East Germany).

You could say that I was not a happy young man on receiving the news, and Val was equally upset. Prior to my moving to Germany, we had talked at great length about our future together. I was delighted to discover that our love for each other was mutual and strong, though in its infancy. We promised each other that we would be there for our mutual support, and I bravely made a vow that I would write to Val every day; she gave me the same promise in return.

The following months were difficult. I settled down in Germany, religiously writing to Val every day, and I eagerly awaited her letters from the UK. I managed to pour my heart out to her in pages of writing every day, and we remained as close as was possible in the circumstances.

Whenever I could, I would get home to her for a few days. I spent hours travelling; by train, Oldenburg to Hoek van Holland, North Sea ferry to Harwich, train to London, train down to Exeter. My love for Val kept me sane on the boring and tedious rail and sea journeys. Luckily, I did sometimes manage to 'hitch' a ride in an RAF plane that was going across to the UK, usually to RAF Lyneham in Wiltshire, which was, of course, in the West Country! When I got to Exeter on the train, there was Val waiting on the platform. I have some wonderful memories of our hugs and kisses on being reunited. The few days we were together strengthened our love, which became deeper still.

My parents saw very little of me at those times; Val and I were inseparable. I would try to surprise Val with a small gift, a token of my love, and I would relate tales of my journey home across several European countries. I remember bringing Val a special gift one day. It was a presentation set of eau de cologne, perfume, soap, powder, etc. I bought it in Cologne or Köln; Val treasured that for years.

There were many simple but lovely adventures we had together during this time and our love stayed strong throughout. We also had many telephone conversations between Germany and Devon. I remember the line was quite strange and echoed, but it was great to hear Val say "I love you" in person!

This situation continued through 1956 and ended unfortunately in an unhappy event. The Soviet Bloc decided to 'rattle its sabre' in Northern Germany by massing tanks and troops on the East German border with West Germany. 300 Signals Unit, including me, were immediately despatched to the border area on Lüneburg Heath – famous in World War 2 as the place where Montgomery took the surrender of Hitler's Northern Army.

It was December 1956 and I had the shattering experience of the northern German winter weather; freezing cold, snow, the coldest I've ever been in my whole life! Christmas came and went. I spent that time in an army barracks in Lüneburg. My Christmas dinner was a large fry-up courtesy of Army Mess cooks, in between nights and days in forests looking at radar screens, and all this time, bitterly cold.

Val coped well with the sudden cancellation of any leave or communication. I managed to let her know that I would be incommunicado for several weeks. She understood that I couldn't tell her too much because of the Official Secrets Act. We did eventually ease down as the military situation improved, and we enjoyed extra leave at home in late February 1957. As I told Val that I loved her, holding her in my arms, we both hoped that we would not have another nightmare Christmas again.

The Christmas 1956 experience in Germany, no letters or phone calls, the tension and the stress for both of us, took its toll. We began to think much more that we needed to be together all of the time. We both talked quite openly about these feelings. Having come through all this, our physical love was, naturally, developing. Nothing too drastic, of course; Val was a lady! With the increased sexual attraction and the excitement it engendered, parting became even more difficult!

Although when I was on leave there were ample opportunities for advancing my sexual desires with Val, I consciously refrained. We 'made do' with cuddles, kisses and some minor 'petting'. She was a virgin and too precious a love for me to take advantage of her. There were plenty of times when she was receptive and it would have been easy for me, but I could not do it. I loved her too much.

One event that was significant in January 1957 was Val's birthday on the 21st. I was in Germany and I could not get any leave. Her parents must have sensed that they were going to lose Val to me and that she would leave the family home. This would be frightening for them because Valerie was the only thing that kept their marriage together. She was the peacemaker, who literally on a daily basis was the only reason the family home stayed intact. I learned much later in our marriage the true extent of the life that Val had endured as a child and through her teens. From physical abuse by her father, to living in a home where there were daily rows and violence between her parents. She had to put up with living a real nightmare, as a child, and she told me that she often had to come between her fighting parents, to physically separate them, and she had to duck to avoid missiles being thrown. She told me that she had felt so alone at this time in her life; the mental scars were with her throughout her life.

During these courting days, Val frequently let me know that her mother, in particular, did not want her to leave the family home. It was clear that her mother thought that without Val there, their marriage would not survive. She told her daughter on many occasions, and she also tried to persuade Val that marriage was not all that it was made out to be. She warned her that she would not be happy, that having children was not a pleasant experience, and she even suggested that I was not suitable for her. It would have been the same for any boyfriends, of course.

The thought of losing Val prompted her parents to offer her a choice for her 21st birthday. She was offered a sum of money or a party. Val chose the party but unfortunately I could not be there. I still have a photograph of Val that she sent to me in Germany, taken at her 21st party. She put a kiss on the back of it in lipstick – another wonderful memory!

Val had many other photos of her party, which I have kept safely today. Thinking back, it was one occasion when I experienced the emotion of jealousy. I could not attend the party, my beloved Val was trying to be happy, surrounded by friends and family, and I could not be part of it. Jealousy at such a time is not a very pleasant feeling. However, I spoke to Val on the telephone from Germany; we pledged our love for each other. We consoled ourselves that at least one important milestone had arrived. She was now twenty-one and an adult in the eyes of the law. The significance of this was clear to both of us. We were free to take our love further. Despite strong opposition to any thought of marriage from her parents, we were now able to further those ideas of being together that we had already talked about secretly.

Our first meeting after her birthday took place in February 1957 when I arrived home on leave. After a lovely few days together, Val and I began to talk privately of taking our romance further. Inevitably, I went down on one knee and proposed to Val. It was in a park locally in Exeter; she was sitting on a bench. She said "yes" when I proffered the ring! We celebrated our engagement in a Chinese restaurant in North Street, Exeter that evening, just the two of us. Our parents' reaction was predictable. My parents were happy and even managed to find glasses and some sherry for a toast – this in an anti-drink home! Val's parents were devastated. As already mentioned, they didn't want Val to leave their home, no matter what, but thank God, my darling Val was adamant; she loved me and that was all that mattered.

Sadly, in the immediate weeks after our engagement, her parents did all they could to break us up and sow seeds of doubt in Val. At the very least, Val's parents hoped to delay our marriage. Val told me about many unpleasant things that happened at this time. Unfortunately, Val had to endure more unhappiness and pain at a time when she should have been very happy. I vowed, once again, that I would do all in my power to make Val happy, eventually as my wife.

It is said that the Almighty moves in mysterious ways His wonders to perform. He certainly did many times in our wonderful and long marriage. While Val was suffering daily opposition to getting married at home, an unusual occurrence made our marriage more possible and more likely.

Val's assistant at Currys, Jeanette Ford, mentioned to Val that her brother and his wife were trying to sell their small terraced house in St David's, quite close to Val's home. The price was good and they wondered if Val and John would be interested, now that they were engaged.

At this time, early in 1957, Val's mother had already embarked on what I see now was a strategy to improve her life if the worst scenario came about, that is, that her daughter got married and left home. It must have been very traumatic for her to anticipate a life alone with her husband, Val's father.

The very presence of Val in the home as a young adult had meant that her previously abusive and frequently violent father's actions were controlled and impossible. Her mother had a natural business acumen. She had learned through necessity to look after her own finances and to manage situations that could arise suddenly without warning in the home. Over a period of time, she asserted herself more and made some shrewd business moves independently of her husband. She purchased some caravans for letting at Dawlish Warren, some beach huts and a chalet at Shutterton Lane, named 'Seaview' – this chalet was to play a special role in our love story!

Val's mother had been helped and supported in this new drive for her own security and independence by her older sister, Beatrice. Valerie's Aunt Beat was already a successful businesswoman in her own right. Together with her husband, Jim Major, they owned and ran a very profitable small shop on St David's Hill and they lived in a lovely bungalow in a desirable area of the city in Sussex Close, St Thomas. Beatrice Major was very supportive of her younger sister, Emily, Val's mum. She was also aware of the problems in Emily's marriage and she did not care for Val's father.

Aunt Beat was also aware of the life that Val had endured for many years. She had a great affection for her niece and this was quite naturally reciprocated by Valerie herself. There was another factor that made the bond between Val and her Aunt Beat even stronger. Jim and Beat Major had one child, a boy called Geoffrey. Val got on well with Geoffrey and they spent time playing together in their early years. Val welcomed the chance to be with her cousins, as it gave her some respite from her own violent and unhappy home.

Tragedy struck, however, when Geoffrey drowned in the River Exe when playing with other children. He was just eight years old. This was another frightening and sad event for the young Valerie to experience, and it would also leave its mark on her in later life. Val's Aunt Beat was also to play an important role in our love story!

Hearing about the available small terraced cottage in St David's, Val and I became very excited. We were now engaged, and the chance of having somewhere to live independently was certainly very attractive and exciting.

There was only one problem. Ken and Pam Ford wanted cash for the cottage and the sale had to be quickly completed. Although we had started saving for our future together, there was no way that we could afford the purchase price, so what to do? Val approached her mother for some financial help by way of a loan to us; we knew that she had some funds from her new business ventures. When her mother declined to help, Val was upset but not at all surprised. She did not want her daughter to get married, after all. This is where Val's Aunt Beat played her role in our love story. She offered us virtually the whole purchase price of the cottage as a loan without interest, to be repaid monthly to her.

This kind gesture was so important in our love story. Aunt Beat knew the life that Val had been through already. She knew also that Val had been close to her lost son and she wanted her niece to have the chance of a new life with a husband to love her, to take care of her and to give her all she deserved. Naturally, I had to be checked out, and I dutifully took tea at the luxury bungalow. I answered all the questions posed by Val's aunt, with a very nervous Valerie sitting by my side. Luckily, or more likely by divine interference, I passed muster!

Aunt Beat told Valerie that she approved of her choice of fiancé and that she would gladly lend us the money to buy the cottage. We walked away from the bungalow that day holding hands and feeling over the moon! We now had no reason to delay our marriage.

Although Val's parents still objected to us marrying, they could not stop us. We were both twenty-one and we now had the prospect of having our own home: a little two-bedroom terraced cottage, 34 Bonhay Road, St David's, Exeter. This was to be our first married home together.

There was one minor problem: Queen's Regulations demanded that I had to formally apply to my Commanding Officer for permission to get married, and my CO was in Germany!

In order to buy the house we had to move quickly, so we started to make plans. A date was set; the marriage would be in October. Accepting that we were not going to change our minds, Val's parents reluctantly agreed to pay for the wedding reception, providing we married in church. There would be difficulties in getting marriage banns called, as I had to return to Germany right away to seek formal permission to marry. This problem was solved when I paid for and obtained a 'Special Licence' from the Bishop of Exeter to marry in one of his churches without banns being called.

This was the start of a very busy time for Val and me during the months leading up to October 1957. I was still stationed in Germany, now at 450 Signals Unit based at NATO HQ, Mönchengladbach near Cologne. This was in the warmer part of Germany at least! I don't know how I did it, but I managed to get an awful lot of leave passes in those few weeks before October. Love can work wonders!

During leave at home with Val in September 1957, in the middle of frantic plans for our wedding, our love story moved significantly on in a very special way. The cottage had been bought and we were busy preparing it as our first home.

We had already visited Seaview, Val's mother's chalet in Shutterton Lane, Dawlish, on one occasion. It had been a brief visit. Val wanted to show me around the holiday let and I was quite impressed with it. Now we were again hurrying from Val's home over to the railway station. We were on our way to Dawlish again to the chalet. I was struggling to carry several large cases and bags containing various household articles, clean sheets, towels, and so on. To help her mum, Val had volunteered to prepare the chalet for a letting in the coming week. Ever trying to be the caring daughter, she was keen to keep her mother as happy as possible, knowing we were only six weeks from our wedding.

After a short journey, we got off the train at Dawlish Warren and walked up to Shutterton Lane. Val, equipped with dusters, cleaning materials and tins of polish, unlocked the chalet. I was pleased to see how clean it was. Looking around, it was clear that there was little cleaning or tidying to do there; the whole place was already immaculate. I sat in the armchair and watched Val change the bedding and briefly polish and dust an already spotless chalet. It had a double bedroom, a bathroom with a full-size bath, a small kitchen area and the lounge area where I was still sitting in a very comfortable armchair.

After a short while, Val had done all that she had to do and joined me in the lounge area. A few minutes later, she was sitting on my lap and in my arms. We began to embrace and kisses followed. For twenty minutes or so we stayed there then Val broke away from me and said, "I'll make us a cup of tea." With that, she went off to the kitchen area. I remember the details vividly to this day.

The Calor gas-heated kettle took some time to boil, so I got up myself and wandered into the bedroom. I was admiring the results of Val's bed-making skills when I felt her presence behind me. I turned and pulled her to me and we began kissing again. To say that I was excited would be an understatement!

The difference this time was that Val was equally aroused and excited. I could feel it in her whole body, in her lips and in her trembling hands that held me tightly against her. I was not consciously aware that things were, at last, moving on in our physical relationship, but they were. We fell back onto the bed and made love for the first time.

Although sexually very excited and full of passionate desire for Val's body, I was very, very gentle with her, slowly moving stage by stage. I knew that she was a virgin and I was determined that this would be special for her. I was so glad that I was experienced in what I was doing. I even had to slow my now eager lover at times, and with difficulty. I managed to take my time.

In truth, I wanted it to be very special for her and it was. Eventually, it was over. It was obvious that Val had experienced great pleasure. She was clinging to me. If I moved, she pulled me back closer to her, and it was some time before we were simply lying there together side by side on the bed. In a semi-clothed state, we stayed there for some time before I was suddenly overcome with disturbing feelings of guilt.

I took her in my arms again and tried to tell her how sorry I was that I had taken advantage of her and that I wished it hadn't happened. We had both known sexual arousement before during some of our long embraces and heavy petting, but we had agreed to wait until we were married. There were only six weeks to go. For a few moments, I was quite upset, even ashamed, with myself. Val's reaction, however, quickly made such thoughts vanish.

She held me close. Kissing me again and again, she assured me that it was okay. It had been wonderful for her, she told me over and over again. It was quite clear that she had experienced some sort of orgasm; she felt good about it all. We hadn't used any form of contraception because it had been so spontaneous, natural and good. 'What if', I suddenly thought, Val became pregnant? That was another worrying thought.

Eventually, we got up from the bed and still feeling guilty, I managed to make two cups of tea. We sipped the tea, holding hands and gazing into each other's eyes. That marvellous day at Seaview did not end with our first intimacy. We stayed there for several more hours. We didn't repeat our love-making but when Val decided to have a bath, things took another step forward!

She didn't lock or even shut the door of the small bathroom and I couldn't resist it! I decided to have a sneaky peek! Val laughed loudly and told me I could 'come in'! I just stood there, looking down at my darling Val, completely naked, for the first time in my life.

She splashed the bathwater playfully and beamed. She looked lovely and, seeing her so happy and smiling up at me, I simply bent over and gave her what I hoped was the most loving kiss I could muster! Then decency took over. I turned and left the bathroom, gently closing the door behind me.

While Val was still in the bathroom, I sat down in the armchair and began to reflect on what had happened that day. I was quite experienced. There was no doubt in my mind that this was different, this was an experience that was new to me. The others had been purely sexual attraction. This was very different. After sixty-one years of marriage, I can confirm that having sex with the woman you love and adore is far more wonderful than any casual affair can be. True love is certainly a splendid thing!

On our journey back to Exeter, we talked in whispers about what had happened. Val was glowing. She was radiant and happy. I still had my guilt-ridden thoughts. I kept apologising in different ways, but Val would not have any of it. She was delighted, happy, and had no feelings of guilt or sadness. I assured her that it wouldn't happen again until we were married, but all she did was tell me that it was all right.

She was glad it had happened and she kept thanking me for being so gentle with her. It had been a lovely and special day for her. I had known for more than eighteen months that I was deeply in love with Val. Our kisses had been special, different and wonderful. I had known that for some time. Now it was plain to see that our love consummated and intimate, at last, was a gift from the

Almighty. I didn't know then that it would grow and develop into a sixty-one-year marriage of sheer wonder and happiness!

Since that day at Seaview chalet in September 1957, the first time Val and I made love together, I have never slept with any other woman. I have been faithful to Valerie and I know that she was faithful to me. She was, and still is, the love of my life, and that is something wonderful, enduring and marvellous.

The six weeks after that special day at Seaview are a somewhat hazy memory for me now. They were days of frantic activity. I returned to my RAF duties in Germany while Val was engaged in a variety of tasks. She was working full time and at the same time trying to prepare for her wedding. She was also working hard at preparing our newly purchased cottage to be our first home together. In later years, I often asked her how she managed to do so much and still remain calm and collected. Her usual reply involved expressions of love and delight at being able to live through such exciting times in her life. She took it all in her stride.

Frequent telephone conversations between Val and me, between Germany and Exeter, did help. She would keep me up to date with all the arrangements, ask for my opinion on various decisions she was called upon to make and tell me she 'loved me dearly!'

Having obtained our special wedding licence and permission to marry from my CO, I was trying to obtain the vital leave pass for mid-October. Like most things, it ended in a compromise. The leave pass to cover the date 26th October 1957 was obtained, but I had to return to my RAF post by the 30th of October. As a result, we would only have four days after our wedding for a honeymoon! To add to the problems, at least a day of that would be taken up with travel time for me to get back to Germany! I broke this news to Val by telephone and she did have a little cry. We agreed that the most important thing was our wedding day, so Val reluctantly accepted my offer of a delayed honeymoon.

When I arrived home for my wedding leave, I realised just how frantic and stressful things had been for Val. Not getting a lot of co-operation from her parents, she had had to shoulder all the responsibility. Somehow, it was all done. The hall, catering, photos, taxis and flowers were all arranged and booked. Invitations had been printed and sent. My darling Valerie had worked wonders, and it had taken its toll.

Three days before the wedding, we were having a quiet drink in a city centre bar when Val suddenly began to get upset. She was quite distressed and angry, mainly with herself, it seemed. I could not understand it at the time, but it had obviously been too much for her over the weeks. Trying to remain calm, I stayed silent and we left the bar. Walking down a narrow and empty Gandy Street, I held her hand. That was when it happened! She suddenly turned to me and let out a torrent of words, all nonsense and incomprehensible. She then pulled away from me and, struggling, she took off her engagement ring and threw it at me! She stomped off away from me and walked away rapidly.

There were no other people in sight as I scrambled on all fours to retrieve the ring. Grabbing the precious ring,

I set off after Val. I caught up with her quite quickly, so she must have slowed down considerably, and on purpose! I pulled her to me and held her tightly. She was shaking, sobbing and very upset, but I could clearly hear the words 'I'm sorry' over and over and over again. I put my arms around her and we slowly made our way into Queen Street. Arriving at the entrance to Northernhay Park, I guided her gently through the park gates and we sat down on a park bench.

Three days before our wedding, I needed some answers quickly. We talked and talked. It was clear that all the excitement, the endless preparations and working full time had been too much for Val. I hugged her and kissed her, dried her tears and soothed her when she constantly apologised. To my eternal relief, when I held out my hand with her engagement ring in it, she grabbed it and hastily returned it to her left-hand finger. We stayed there on that bench for more than an hour. When we got up, the episode was over, and I walked her home with my arm around her.

On that walk down to Val's home in St David's, I could not escape the nagging thoughts going through my mind. Had she now changed her mind about marrying me? Did she have doubts? Was this the beginning of the end for us? As we neared Tavistock Road and her home, I could wait no longer. I had to know the answers to those questions. We stopped in our usual place and I took her in my arms. She seemed calmer. She looked up at me and smiled. I kissed her. It was an important kiss for me and I put everything I could into it! After a long and delightful kiss, I whispered the questions to her. She pulled me to her and told me that she loved me. She said that she must have suffered what many brides-to-be suffer, just before their wedding: 'wedding nerves' or something of the sort. I just stood there staring into her eyes as she looked up at me. After what seemed like an eternity, I knew that it was fine; all would be well on Saturday, our Wedding Day.

Chapter 3

Wedded Bliss

Saturday 26th October 1957 at 12.00 noon, Val and I were married at St David's Church, Exeter. The church was full. Friends and family members from far and wide, and even a few interested members of the public, witnessed our wedding. It was a traditional Anglican ceremony according to the Solemnization of Matrimony rites of the Book of Common Prayer 1662 with various amendments.

I was nervous standing there with my best man, Glenn, and true to tradition, Valerie was just a couple of minutes late! What my darling Val was thinking as she walked up the aisle, I will never know. She was, after all, on the arm of her father, who was responsible for her unhappy childhood. She was a devout Christian and throughout the ceremony, the reception and the whole day, she gave no indication of any upset, worry or concerns regarding those earlier troubled days of her life. She looked very happy, a truly radiant bride. The ceremony went without a hitch and I still remember clearly when I responded to the vicar's words, "You may kiss the bride." A beautiful but short kiss!

Many times during our marriage, Val would tease me about one of the things that she did think about as she walked up the aisle towards me. She was convinced that she could see my trouser creases shaking as she approached me! Evidently, my legs were shaking as I tried to maintain my military-style 'attention' pose!

The wedding went well and everyone concerned, particularly close family members, did their bit in maintaining the appropriate decorum required. As we left the church, we were assailed by a cloud of confetti. I gripped Val's hand tightly and made a silent vow to do my best to love, honour and cherish my new wife. I would do all that I could to make Val's life as happy as it could be. I was aware that many who witnessed our wedding did not know about Val's childhood, including close family on both sides. I knew, however, and a few others also knew or had suspicions of their own.

Writing this, sixty-one years later, I am drawn to the memories in particular of our marriage vows given to each other on that day. I have reread those same vows carefully, several times. A rather battered copy of the Book of Common Prayer is beside me now and I feel a warm glow in knowing that I did all in my power over the sixty-one years to fulfil my vows, and she did the same.

"Wilt thou love her, comfort her, honour and keep her, in sickness and in health, and forsaking all other, keep thee only unto her, so long as ye both shall live?"

I answered clearly, "I will," and I believe I did so throughout a long and happy sixty-one years and four months.

The wedding reception went well also. It was held at the old wartime canteen building on what is now a large car park in front of St David's Station. I must give credit to Val's parents for an excellent reception. No expense was spared and it was well planned. It was as if her parents had accepted the inevitable that Valerie would be leaving them, for me. I have a lovely memory of my grandparents at the reception. They loved Val so much and had appreciated all the love and care that she had shown to them. To see this old couple smile and bless our union meant a great deal to Val and I. It warms my heart to this day.

Knowing that we only had a few days before I had to return to my RAF duties in Germany, Val and I had decided to make sure we did not travel too far for our short honeymoon. We kept it a secret, of course!

Our parents, Val's bridesmaid Muriel Salter, and others saw us off on the train at St David's Station. It was bound for London Paddington. Val, resplendent in a new two-piece outfit, and I, in a smart new suit, waved to the assembled crowd on the platform as we started our journey. What the guests did not know then was that we were to get off the train at the second stop, namely at Taunton in Somerset! We got off the train clutching our cases. It was still a lovely sunny day and we took a taxi to our destination for the next two days: the Rose Inn on the outskirts of Taunton. This was a detached olde-worlde inn and B&B run by an ex-RAF flight lieutenant and his wife. We were welcomed with understanding and great friendliness by our hosts and shown up to the best room in the inn with the expected 'knowing' smiles!

After a few lengthy hugs and kisses in our room, we changed into more casual clothes and set off on foot for the town centre to get an evening meal. We decided against going into many restaurants on the grounds that they were too crowded. Eventually, we found a rather old-fashioned, dusty and somewhat run-down restaurant with only one couple already there. We ate a good meal and giggled a lot when we took in the restaurant's décor. There were stuffed animals in glass cases around the room. The tables, cutlery and serviettes were all from a different age, but all very clean. It was as if this place hadn't changed much from the last century, but it certainly remained in our memories for sixty or more years. We were so very happy as we walked hand in hand back to the Rose Inn for our Wedding Night.

All these years later, I have discovered a reference to this restaurant and our wedding night in one of Val's diaries. I have been loath to read many of Val's diaries since her death because they were private and her secret thoughts. This one entry, however, caught my eye, and I am now glad that I read it. It was written on our thirty-eighth wedding anniversary here in Dawlish. In it, Val wrote that we had decided to go for a walk, having a quiet day of celebration together. I will quote from Val's diary:

We had a nice walk. John wore his blazer. We sat down on a seat overlooking the sea. John kissed me. We started to think back and talked about the

early days, about the Rose Inn and that restaurant.
We walked home hand in hand. It was a lovely day.

My darling Val had written those words on a day thirty-eight years into our marriage, a superb reminder to me now of happy days. I do feel sure that the Almighty had a hand in this. Why should it be this single diary entry that caught my eye in these grieving sad days? Reading it some months after Val's passing gave me a warm feeling of that deep love, once again.

On returning to the Rose Inn, we had a glass of wine together in the busy lounge bar and slipped away up to our room before 10 pm. Our wedding night is forever fixed in my memory. Although we had already made love once at Seaview some six weeks earlier, this was a very special night because we were now husband and wife. Undressing together for the first time ever, I was amazed to see that Val did not appear to be shy. She was happy and not at all embarrassed. There was a full-length mirror in the wardrobe of the room and we stood there, arms around one another, completely naked, and for several minutes adored the view of each other's bodies. We did eventually put on nightclothes and I told Val how lovely she looked in her flimsy new nightdress before we climbed into the large double bed. Our marriage was truly consummated with great physical pleasure and much love. We fell asleep closely wrapped in each other's arms. It was a superb fairy-tale end to a very special day for us.

Our short but wonderful honeymoon lasted only two days at the Rose Inn in Taunton. We were back in Exeter late on the Sunday evening. We stayed with my parents that night and we were naturally on our best behaviour!

I desperately wanted to continue the love-making from the previous night as soon as we went to bed. Val would have none of it, however. She rejected my advances. "They'll hear us," she was constantly reminding me, so I had to be content with a night of cuddles and whispers! Luckily, we were both tired out and fell asleep quickly in each other's arms.

After a splendid breakfast prepared with pride by my mother, we began to think about the tasks ahead of us. We had the key to our new home, our cottage in Bonhay Road, and I had one day left of my leave from the RAF. There was a lot to do. I dimly remember the chaos that ensued that day. We managed to get to our cottage by taxi and I put the cases down outside the front door. As the taxi pulled away, I turned to Val. She was standing there in her lovely lilac outfit, smiling at me. I looked into her eyes and it was such a delight to see the love and affection there.

I managed to unlock the front door and with one swift movement I picked Val up and carried her through the small doorway and into our first home. It was a good job that I was over six foot tall and twelve and a half stone and that Val was only five foot one and around seven stone! I managed to deposit Val on the sofa that I found in the small living room and she threw her arms around me as we kissed. It was a good five minutes before we pulled apart and surveyed our new home for the first time together.

Val had been extremely busy in the weeks before our wedding. Although working full time, she had put up curtains, supervised the arrival of our first suite of furniture, arranged for lino to be laid, mats, and so on. The tiny kitchen had a small cooker, crockery and some saucepans, and hot water, electricity and gas were connected. She had done wonders. As she took me on a guided tour of the small house, she beamed at her handiwork with considerable pride. The faded wallpaper and décor were hardly noticed as we admired the large old-fashioned bed that Val had bought and put up in the main bedroom. The other small bedroom was full of suitcases and a miscellany of household items. She was so proud of her achievement in managing to set up a home for the first time, it brought me close to tears as I lavished praise on her, and quite a few hugs and kisses!

After the initial euphoria had eased a little and we began to warm up a rather damp cottage with the help of a large brand-new electric fire in the living room, Val made me her first-ever meal and we tried to plan our next tasks. There was so much to do and think about. My own thoughts were dominated by a constant reminder that I was due back at RAF Mönchengladbach in Germany the following day. Understandably, Val did not want to think about that!

I managed to sort out some clothes and pack a holdall that day ready for the journey. Meanwhile, Val seemed to spend hours dusting, polishing and washing every corner of her new small home.

The following day, I set off on my journey back to the RAF in Germany. It was our first parting as a married couple, albeit married only a few days. Val was in tears waving me off from a bleak St David's Station platform.

The euphoria of getting married and spending a night in our new home soon wore off as my train hastened towards London Paddington. Looking at my tickets, I realised that I had completely forgotten that due to the rapidly approaching Autumn Equinox, British Summer Time would end. This meant the railway and boat timetables would also change!

It rapidly dawned on me that I would miss the Continental Boat from Harwich and as a result I would also be at least a day late back at my RAF base in Germany. I would be officially 'absent without leave'! Mobile phones and the internet were simply science fiction in those days. There was no way I could avoid it. I did manage to let Val know, via her mother's telephone, from Paddington Station. There were some tears but I ploughed on with the journey to Harwich with some trepidation.

Eventually arriving at my base in Mönchengladbach, I awaited the dreaded call. It came the following day. The CO wanted to see me at 10.00 hours! After listening to the Wing Commander's rather lengthy tirade, which seemed to cover all of the Queen's Regulations at the time, he asked why I was AWOL. I told him that I had got married on the previous Saturday and then sheepishly explained about British Summer Time and the timetable. I thought I heard him mutter, "Your mind was on other things, I suppose," and I am sure that there was a slight smile on his face as he bellowed, "Dismissed – get out of here!" As I saluted, turned and almost ran to his door, he added, "Congratulations, by the way."

That evening, I wrote a long letter to Val. It was full of all the events but was mainly a love letter telling her that I missed her so much! The next few weeks went by quickly and were quite eventful. I wrote love letters to Val on a daily basis and in November I received some great news. I was to be posted back to the UK and, best of all, I was going to be stationed at 229 OCU, RAF Chivenor in North Devon, just over forty miles from my home and my beloved wife!

Luckily, I guess the RAF bureaucratic HQ at Innsworth in Gloucestershire wanted all the paperwork done and dusted before Christmas. This resulted in my early departure for Chivenor, and I was able to be home in time for Christmas. The statuary posting leave meant that Val and I were able to enjoy our first Christmas together as a married couple in our new home in Exeter. What a wonderful Christmas it was too, a couple of weeks of bliss and happiness together.

Val loved having her own little house and I was happy putting up curtain rails, painting and doing various other maintenance chores. The only problem we had was that we discovered some other residents in the house: a family or two of mice! The cottage had been empty for some time before we moved in and it soon became clear that the mice had taken over! There was only one real answer. We had to get a cat. That presented us with another problem. I had been brought up with cats and dogs in my home; Val had only had a dog. I soon discovered that Val's mother could not stand cats and was in fear of them. This phobia about cats had been passed on to Val.

We discussed the situation for several days while trying other methods to move the mice. Val was adamant and this was our first minor disagreement ever. Using all the cunning I could muster, I kept on about the mess the mice left around the place and the scratching noises at night. Val finally gave in when she saw the mice at close quarters once or twice! I got the required approval at last. Visiting the local RSPCA, I returned with a lovely one-year- old female cat called 'Fluffy'. She had been rescued from a farm in Crediton. On entering our sitting room, Fluffy spotted Val sitting in an armchair, rushed over and jumped up onto her lap. Val froze in panic. For a moment, I was worried, but Fluffy settled down and fell asleep. Within minutes, she was purring contentedly. This was a significant day in Val's life. We had Fluffy for fifteen years and she grew to love cats. We had cats in all our homes for most of our married years, after that. Within days, I should add, Fluffy had cleared the cottage of mice and I spent the final few days of my leave disposing of them. This cat was also to be great company for Val when I was away during the rest of my RAF service.

Chapter 4

Married Life in the RAF

From the day we got married on 26th October 1957 until the date of my discharge on 22nd February 1967, Val was the wife of a serviceman. We did not really control our lives together. Everything we did was governed by an authority greater than us. The Royal Air Force was all-powerful and we were only able to make minor decisions. Where I would be living, what I could do, and my every movement was dictated by the RAF. As a result, Val had to face a new learning experience every day. Although in the early weeks of our marriage this was difficult for her, she coped well. She continued with her own career working full time, she managed to establish a lovely little home for us, and she supported me in every way possible. We simply loved each other so much that we both worked hard to ensure that we were as happy as we could be in the circumstances.

Strange as it may seem, when I look back now, in many ways it was an ideal start to our marriage. We were apart for many days and often weeks at a time. Throughout all of these nine or so years, it was truly a case of 'absence makes the heart grow fonder'.

There were so many occasions when we were separated for a while. When we did meet up again, it was just like our courting days all over again! Val would be waiting for me on the platform of a railway station, often St David's in Exeter, and we would run into each other's arms and the excitement and love would overcome everything else! We had so many fresh 'honeymoon' weekends on a regular basis that it was quite wonderful, although exhausting for us both.

During those years of service marriage, there were many special times. Val often travelled to meet me at an RAF station, a London rail station and, once or twice, at an RAF hospital! There were also times when we were together for longer periods. Val spent some time in Cornwall when I was at St Mawgan, and we enjoyed more than two years actually living together in Singapore; more of that later. Being apart so much ensured that we certainly made the most of the times when we were together. Val carried on her career in music and bookselling, so she had some independence. This meant that she retained contact with her circle of female friends socially and, in fact, she could almost continue with a 'single' life in many ways. I hasten to add, without too much male company!

Surprisingly, in view of her troubled childhood, she also did her best to keep her parents together. While maintaining her own independence and our home, she was able to visit her parents and mine on a regular basis when I was away. Val's life during these years was a very busy one. She didn't really have time to get upset or down about anything. She was working hard; she had good loyal female friends; she had a home to run; parents to visit and who visited her. She had me to think about or worry about; she had letters to write to me or telephone calls to make; but she could look forward to 'honeymoon' meetings with me regularly.

All in all, looking back, our first nine years of marriage were in some ways an ideal scenario for us. It certainly gave us a sound basis for many years to come. I mentioned above some special times during our 'service years', and these do need some further explanation. Singapore and my illnesses come to mind!

In our marriage, we quickly established a routine after my posting to RAF Chivenor. I was now just over forty miles from Val and I could virtually guarantee our weekends together. The new base I was on was an operational training base, not a frontline operational one. Using every ploy and trick in the book, I made sure that most Friday evenings I could be seen signing out of Chivenor and then heading up the road to Val and our home in Exeter! I can recall on occasions spending many pounds bribing some of my colleagues to do my weekend duties for me. These were mostly single chaps who were glad of the money; it was definitely worth every penny! It allowed me to spend idyllic weekends with Val; weekends when we could continue our love affair and be very happy. There was also, of course, the added bonus of my laundry being lovingly attended to by Val and enjoying her rapidly improving culinary skills. This situation continued for a year or two, punctuated by a few notable incidents.

One weekend, I suffered an accident while at home. The origins are unclear to this day, but the result was a spinal seizure that found me collapsed on the stairs of our home, unable to move and in terrible pain. Quickly getting over the initial shock of finding me like this, Val was superb in her first aid. With her help, I managed to get to our bedroom and wait for medical help to arrive. Eventually, after visits from our GP and an orthopaedic consultant, a PID was diagnosed (prolapsed intervertebral disc). This resulted in more than a week in bed flat on my back and in due course a visit to the local hospital for further treatment. Two weeks later, I walked out of hospital wearing a plaster jacket, plaster from my shoulders to my hips! Some good things did come of this injury, however! I ended up at home with my beloved Val for six weeks or so! The plaster cast I was wearing did inhibit movement, of course. Nevertheless, Val and I were very inventive in bed and she was able to ensure that my recovery was aided by an extremely loving carer!

I returned to my duties in the RAF at Chivenor for the following two years or so. Val and I continued to live apart for five days of each week, spending the weekends, Friday to Monday morning, together in what became very happy occasions. We talked on the telephone most evenings during the week. Val would update me on her workdays and we would try to plan our weekend activities. It worked well. Every weekend was a new adventure for us in our love affair, exciting and happy times that I remember well. We had three nights together and our love was nourished and grew with the opportunities these weekends presented. The days seemed to fly by and we built up a routine that worked well for us and our marriage.

Val also had our cat Fluffy to look after. Fluffy would always be eagerly awaiting Val's arrival home from work. In fact, most days she would leave her workplace and rush home at lunchtimes, grabbing a sandwich and feeding the cat. I managed to install a cat flap in our back door so that Fluffy had easy access to the house. Val was quite happy just working, spoiling the cat weekdays and spoiling me at weekends! Absence makes the heart grow fonder, they say, and this was certainly true for the two of us in these years of our marriage. Looking back now, I do believe that these circumstances helped build a sound base for the many happy years in our marriage that were to come, as I have said before.

All good things come to an end, however, and our idyllic lifestyle took a blow when the RAF decided to post me to RAF Tengah, because this operational fighter station was located many thousands of miles away in Singapore!

Val was terribly upset on hearing news of my posting. The first weekend after I received my posting, we didn't go anywhere. It was spent in bouts of crying from Val, and me trying to console her. I wasn't too happy myself, of course, but I tried to hide my feelings from her and use all my ingenuity to 'talk up' the good things that might be possible. Holding her close, I told her that there was every chance that she would be able to join me in Singapore. We could live together in married quarters.

"I couldn't do that," she cried, clutching Fluffy the cat to her. "It's the other side of the world."

We had three more weeks of increasingly depressing weekends together before a week of embarkation leave. Eventually, the day arrived when I had to say my tearful farewells, and I set off on my journey to Singapore. We had managed to improve our personal feelings about the posting a little during the week of my leave. We were still very much in love and we clung to each other and pledged our love all over again with much fervour and sincerity. Our love will see us through, we told each other. I do believe this was the first time that Val thought about trying to persuade me to abandon my RAF career and become a civilian, at home with her!

Most of my spare time on the journey to Singapore was spent writing postcards and short letters to Val, telling her to be strong and how much I missed her already! This was a time before all the modern communication systems that exist today. Quick phone conversations, email messages and instant voice communication were the stuff of dreams. It was 'snail mail' plus the occasional telegram or cable. I do remember sending a telegram to Val from Singapore to say I had arrived safely, following that with a lengthy love letter!

It was about two months into my posting at RAF Tengah and I was already making enquiries about bringing Val out to join me, when I believe that the Almighty intervened! I had noticed during the weeks that I was feeling some pain again in the lumbar region of my back. With clear memories of my disc trouble two years previously, I was quite worried about the increasing pain I was now feeling in my back and my legs. After a few days of putting up with it, I decided to seek professional advice from the medics. It all happened quite quickly over a few days. The pain increased and I eventually found myself bedridden. I could not walk or even stand upright! To be fair, the RAF medical officers were superb. I was quickly transferred from RAF Tengah to RAF Hospital Changi in downtown Singapore. I was flat out in a hospital bed, unable to move, let alone write to my darling Val. The RAF were very good. They sent a cable/telegram to Val and followed this with an explanatory longer cable from the MO in charge. A day or so later, the orthopaedic consultant told me that X-rays had confirmed that the same disc had prolapsed again. Plaster jackets or similar were out of the question in a tropical climate, so there was only one solution: I had to be sent back to the UK, what the military calls 'Casevac' (casualty evacuation). The consultant told me that his friend Wing Commander Povey at RAF Hospital Wroughton near Swindon would hopefully sort out my spinal problems, as he was a Harley Street orthopaedic surgeon!

I mentioned earlier that I believe the Almighty had intervened in my life at this time. I have only thought this in recent years. It does seem rather remarkable that I should have had such a severe medical condition at a time when I was quite young and fit. Also at a time when I was separated by some thousands of miles from the woman I loved so much and who I knew was missing me so much too. The Almighty moves in mysterious ways!

I was on a stretcher, strapped down, and carried out of RAF Hospital Changi, to the waiting Casevac aeroplane at the airport, RAF Changi. It was only a short journey. The specially adapted aircraft was a Comet 4 hospital plane and there were several other unfortunate patients on board apart from me. I remember that I was on my stretcher bed, and opposite me was a Gurkha soldier who was suffering from a brain tumour. He was being flown back from his duties in central Malaya to get treatment in the UK which would save his life. Unfortunately, I was unable to talk to him on the journey, but we did manage to smile at each other across the aisle and shake hands; he only had limited words of English and my Gurkhali is non-existent. I did then think that the British Empire was not all bad!

We patients on this aircraft were well looked-after by Queen Mary RAF nurses, all sisters, and two doctors, RAF MOs. After overnight refuelling stops at Aden and Malta, we eventually touched down at RAF Lyneham in Wiltshire. I was whisked off, still on my stretcher, by ambulance to travel the few miles to the RAF hospital at Wroughton, near Swindon. It is today, I understand, an NHS general hospital for the area.

I awoke the following day still flat out in my hospital bed to a sister telling me that I had a visitor, but that she could only stay for one hour, strict regulations! There, coming through the door into the ward, I could see the truly lovely sight of my darling Val, resplendent in a lilac outfit and smiling broadly! The RAF had cabled Val with details of the Casevac flight and even provided a free travel warrant for her journey up from Exeter.

I remained at Wroughton RAF Hospital for another ten days while the consultant decided on suitable treatment.

They were considering an operation on my spine, a laminectomy, or similar, to fuse the damaged vertebrae. It was not a pleasant thought and I was not keen on having this done, as there were considerable risks involved and the success rate of complete cure was low. My fears about this operation were confirmed when I managed to have a chat at my bedside with an airman medic who had undergone the operation some years previously. The fact that this chap had difficulty in walking and standing upright was enough for me. I was determined to refuse surgery. Luckily, I did not have to make the decision; Wing Commander Povey told me that he had ruled out operating and that he would put me in a plaster jacket, as this had worked for the consultant at the RD&E Hospital in Exeter some two years before. It was with some relief that I gave Val this news when she visited me again a few days later. As always, Val was upbeat and cheerful. On this visit, she had also brought my parents up with her; she had arranged for their journey and paid for their train tickets, taxi and everything. That was the caring nature of my darling wife.

A week or so later, encased in plaster from shoulders to hips, I gingerly got into a taxi and set off for Exeter, my home and my Valerie. The next few weeks were officially 'sick leave' and I enjoyed the delights of being cared for and indulged by Val in our little cottage in Exeter. A cable arrived one day from the RAF; my hands were trembling as I opened it! Val hovered nearby and when I turned, hugged her and gave her a big kiss, she knew it was good news. I had to report back to duty at 229 OCU RAF Chivenor, located just up the road in North Devon; we were both delighted.

For the next couple of years, we reverted to our previous idyllic lifestyle. I would be at Chivenor for five days and then spend Friday to Monday morning with my beloved Val in Exeter. We quickly got back into the routine. The weekend 'honeymoons' took place frequently and life seemed great again. My back condition improved and remained sound after the plaster had been removed, although I had to wear a substantial 'corset support' for some time. I also knew that it would be months or maybe years before I would get another posting, due to my medical downgrading.

During this period, we had some wonderful weekends together and one or two holidays too. We visited some friends and family roots in Perth, Scotland. There, Val was once again my 'star attraction'. My father had been brought up in Scotland, in Perth, until he was ten years old. Before our journey to Perth, as fathers do, he gave us instructions on where to go in his home town, who we had to visit, and he even gave us maps and detailed routes. We had already visited Edinburgh on our belated honeymoon. Once again, we took the first-class rail trip via the *Flying Scotsman* from London. We excitedly relived our previous honeymoon journey. In addition, this time we were able to visit other places in Scotland. Val, always a royalist, was so happy to visit Balmoral, the Queen Mother's home at Glamis... and some of my father's oldest friends. She quickly made an impact on them; she was so delightful in her manners and friendliness. She was so fascinated by the loving reception she got from everyone there. One lady, Marie Wylie, had been a work colleague many years ago of my father's sister, my Aunt Gladys. We looked up this old lady at her small flat in Perth. She was so welcoming as she fussed over us in her flat, pouring tea from her best bone china and insisting that we ate her scones and cake. She suddenly broke down in tears of happiness, just so happy at seeing us and talking to us, happy that we had bothered to look her up. Val comforted her and was glowing with pleasure herself from the sheer joy of the occasion. Val wrote to Marie on a regular basis on our return to Devon. Thinking back now as I write this, I realise how and why Val reacted as she did. It was another small way that her life had improved, through our marriage and through our love.

Another holiday during this time was to Normandy in France. This turned out to be another eventful time for us. We were on a luxury coach trip through Normandy. Arriving for a night's stay in Lisieux, the tour operator told the coach party that two people were not booked into the luxury hotel where we had stopped. It was Val and I! Through some sort of admin error at the travel agent's, we had been left off the list, and we ended up at another hotel in the town. Valerie was not amused! We did have a good holiday in the end, however, and Val ticked off some more of her 'wants list' of dreams. She saw the Bayeux Tapestry and visited the D-Day beaches at Arromanches.

The final few years of my RAF service saw Val and me living in Singapore, where I was once again posted to in 1964. I recall this period of our life together with particular fondness. It was, I am now convinced, the period of our marriage which cemented our love affair;

the foundation of all those wonderful happy years that followed.

Our travels together took a rather important and significant step forward in the year 1964. That was when I was informed that I was being posted overseas again. It was to Singapore. I have already written about my previous trip to the Far East. Then I was travelling alone, although married to Val at the time. That posting was short-lived, as I was flown back to the UK on a stretcher! This time, I was determined that Val would get the travel experience of a lifetime and join me in Singapore. I knew this would not be easy to do, however, on several fronts. Firstly, Val's parents and her family would be opposed to her travelling so far, possibly for years; secondly, Val herself was nervous about such a long flight. She was also worried about her mother's health, which was already failing, and she was under a lot of pressure not to go.

Luckily for me, and for Val, our love and, I am sure, a 'nudge' from the Almighty prevailed. It was another very special time in our life together. It turned out to be the last overseas posting I had in my RAF career, and within a year of returning to the UK from Singapore, I had decided to leave the RAF and embark on a career in teaching. This decision was naturally a joint one made between Val and I after much thought and discussion. Nevertheless, living with me in Singapore, thousands of miles away, on the other side of the world worked wonders for Val. She was able to fulfil many of her private dreams, to live independently with me together, far away from the influence of her parents and the scene of her childhood nightmares. It was an ideal preparation for

Val and me to embark on a new life together in the world outside of the military service. Val had only known me in the RAF; that was soon to change!

I believe that many of Val's family were on the platform at St David's Station, Exeter, to see her off on her journey to join me in Singapore. I had flown out some six weeks before and I had been busy preparing for Val's arrival. I was very excited when I was handed a cable saying that she had taken off from Heathrow Airport and giving me the details, flight number, and so on. I had already rented a flat in the local town close to my new RAF base Seletar. I had enjoyed the pleasures of independent living, cooking for myself and being away from Mess living on base for a couple of weeks. I had even employed an *amah* servant, a young Chinese lady ready to do Val's chores! It was then the twilight days of the British Empire, The Raj, when Brits still retained some pride and old-world privilege. Sipping cold Tiger beers, I spent a few nervous days watching old US TV shows and films and longing to see Val again.

The great day arrived! I was so excited. Having arranged a few days' leave, I showered, shaved and put on a newly bought pair of trousers and a new white shirt. It was a very hot day as usual and I was literally shaking as I got into the taxi at Jalan Kayu, giving the driver instructions to go to Singapore's International Airport at Paya Lebar. I tried to calm myself by thinking of Val and remembering the 'stiff upper lip' British way. It patently didn't work! I ended up throughout the journey talking to the Malay taxi driver and telling him what was going on. He was cheerful and happy for me.

He was even happier when I said that he should wait to pick the two of us up for the return journey and that I would pay for the inevitable waiting time at the airport!

I was naturally too early for Val's flight, so I joined the crowds watching all the aircraft coming and going from an observational balcony. Soon, the waiting was over. At last, I recognised Val's aircraft taxi in, a large four-engine Britannia Airways turbo-prop. I had already written down its route out from London, two stops on the way: overnight in Istanbul, Turkey and Bombay, India. I tried to remain calm as I made my way to the reception area. I spotted Val instantly as she struggled to collect her cases. I crushed her in my arms and kissed her over and over again. She pushed me away eventually, gasping for breath. I finally came to my senses! I had myself flown into Singapore many times and exiting an aircraft there is like walking straight into a baker's oven! What on earth was I thinking! I stood back and looked at Val; she was flushed red and gasping for breath, and then I noticed the large plasters on her upper arms. The various inoculations and jabs she had to endure prior to her trip. I had forgotten all those simple things!

That day when Val arrived in Singapore remains clear in my memory. It was the start of a new and exciting life for us, living together every day as a married couple for the first time. We really started on a new adventure in Singapore and I am convinced it did wonders for our marriage, our love affair and our future together.

During Val's first week with me in Singapore, it soon became clear that she would settle in quickly and enjoy her new life. A friend of mine had already invited us to his bungalow for evening dinner with his wife and children, a welcome party of sorts for us. After only two days in the sweltering climate, Val looked calm and cool as she dressed for dinner. Our hosts were great and they made us most welcome. Val spent a lot of time absorbing information on practical things, advice on where to shop, what to buy and what not to do! The wives of some of my RAF colleagues were all very welcoming and helpful to Val during her first few weeks in the Far East. She was a quick learner; she soon mastered all that was necessary for her to run an apartment home for us in a climate and environment that were new to her. She also had the added support, help and advice from our *amah*, the Chinese girl that I had employed. Val did not have to worry about cleaning our apartment, washing or ironing, shopping, or even the cooking; this was all taken care of by the *amah*! This young Chinese lady, called Foo Soon Lan, got quite annoyed if she found Val doing one of 'her' jobs! The *amah* didn't 'live in', as it was a single-bedroom flat, so Val simply waited until the evenings when we were alone, then she would busy herself around the rooms happily.

We had a comfortable life in the circumstances. Due to the climate, the RAF only expected me to work half a day, each day; sometimes in shifts. As a result, I would often work a morning up to lunchtime and then have free time until the next day. I would be on call at times, but I certainly enjoyed all the leisure time it offered. The RAF bases had swimming pools, and the large ones also had a full-sized cinema and other leisure facilities on base.

Val soon discovered that she could live a life of comparative luxury, thinking of her working life in the UK! She would often leave me a message in the flat or with the *amah* – '*See you at 1400 hours at the pool restaurant*' or sometimes, '*Going shopping in Singapore City with the girls*', meaning other wives she had quickly befriended. She loved it! We joined the RAF Yacht Club and Val learned to sail during the two and a half years we were there. The Yacht Club had its own restaurant with lovely views out over the Straits of Johor. We spent many happy hours as a twosome alone enjoying the amenities there, and also many other times with couples, our friends.

When I now recall those days in the sixties, it is no wonder that our marriage blossomed out there in Singapore. The weather was always hot and sunny, although very humid; ideal weather for a lot of swimming and sailing. It is true that the monsoon season caused us a few problems, but that was quite a short period each year. I remember Val and some friends went sailing on one occasion when I was at work. On this particular day, the weather changed suddenly and they were stuck out in the middle of the Straits of Johor 'in irons', that is, with no wind to get them back to shore. The weather did change eventually when they had a monsoon storm with torrential rain. They got back to the Yacht Club in a terrible state, as they had been exposed to the tropical sun on the yacht with little shelter for several hours. They were all badly sunburnt, including Val. She suffered for several days, being very sick and in so much pain on her skin that she was unable to get up and dress; she had to spend two days lying on her bed with only a cotton sheet over her naked body. Luckily for me, the *amah* took over nursing Val, and she also kept me fed for a few days! That's probably when I took a fancy to Far Eastern food, Malayan curry and Indonesian *nasi goreng*. It was a salutary lesson for Val, however; she would carefully check the weather forecast and always wear suitable clothes and headgear on future outings at sea.

Val became very active as a member of the Anglican Church during our time in Singapore. She joined the church's Guild of Wives on the RAF base, and she manned stalls at fetes and did a lot of charity work with them. They raised money for an orphanage, which was run by some Dutch nuns in Johor State, Malaya. Val often remembered events from our time in the Far East throughout our long marriage. She met the Sultan of Johor, with her church group, on a visit to Malaya. She proudly told me how he had let her sit on his throne in his palace! Certainly something I would never do in my life!

The RAF Anglican padre on the base, the Rev. Thomas, persuaded Val to join his Confirmation classes; this eventually resulted in her Confirmation in the Anglican faith at St George's Church in Singapore on Palm Sunday 1966. I was very proud of her as she was confirmed by the Bishop of Maidstone, with the Bishop of Singapore also in attendance, that day.

Val also improved her culinary skills while in Singapore; she mastered some of the arts of Malay cooking and some Indonesian dishes. This was to last her a lifetime. Many years later, visitors from the UK and overseas friends would comment on Val's Malayan curry dishes with extras! Extras would be everything from chopped raw onions, bananas and raw pineapple to a variety of chutneys from Malaya and various types of nuts and, of course, a special sauce!

We also had some rather splendid outings together as a couple. This included the two of us seeing in the New Year at the famous Raffles Hotel in Singapore and at the large Hotel Singapura. I will not mention some of the other places we visited in downtown Singapore, usually in the early hours, in a state of inebriation, with other couples in tow!

The year 1966 saw us return to the UK together. We enjoyed a once-in-a-lifetime voyage by sea from Singapore to London on the *SS Benloyal*. This journey is recalled in some detail in the next chapter about our travels. Our future life was to take a different direction as a result of the thoughts and discussions that we had started when we were in Singapore. The decision on me leaving the RAF and starting a new career in the teaching profession had really been made. The main driving force for this was the overwhelming desire that we both had to be able to be together for the rest of our lives. In other words, it was driven by love! We desperately wanted to be together and we could not do this if I remained in the RAF. It came to dominate our thoughts every day; the search for a career move for me that would enable us to set up a permanent home and hopefully start a family.

On returning to the UK, I told the RAF of my intentions. I would leave the service as soon as it was possible to do so, subject to any contractual obligations. I had some useful meetings with RAF education officers at my new base, which was back at 42 Squadron, Coastal

Command, at St Mawgan in Cornwall. Luckily, the RAF were very helpful and understanding. They had co-operated by posting me to Cornwall on my return from the Far East. I was quite close to my home in Exeter and I could easily drive up the A30 at weekends. They also gave me all the information I needed to apply for a place at Exeter University in order to obtain a teaching qualification. As 1966 went by, Val and I grew more excited about the possibilities for my future and our future life together, in a settled home. Most of our weekends together during 1966 were spent planning our future. We had settled back into our little cottage in Exeter and we had renewed our loving relationship with Fluffy, our cat. She had been looked after by one of Val's cousins, who had lived in our house with her husband during our time in Singapore. It was good for them as a young married couple to be able to live in our house for a token rent for more than two years, and it suited us, particularly as it allowed Fluffy, our cat, to stay there too!

We did have some problems to overcome in fulfilling our plans. Val had been able to return to her old job as a bookseller, and she was soon back in her working world. I would be able to leave the RAF early the following year, 1967. The problem was that the earliest I could get a place at university for my teaching course was October 1967. It would mean that I would be without employment for more than six months. Val assured me that we would manage financially but I was not so sure! She offered to get a second job herself and she kept reminding me that we didn't have any rent to pay, providing we stayed in our little terraced house. She desperately wanted me at home with her and she was sure that we could manage. I made the appropriate application for a local government grant to cover my university course; I attended the university selection procedures and interviews and we were both delighted when these were both successful. I was offered a university place and I then had written confirmation of the grant from the county council. To be honest, we were both quite shocked when we realised just how little money we would have to live on! At the time, teachers were desperately needed and the Government was running a recruitment campaign. When Val and I did the sums, we realised that our total income would be about a quarter of what we had been used to, including Val's salary working full time!

We were becoming increasingly worried that the viability of our plans was in doubt; we spent anxious weekends discussing it all. Val was marvellous, as she always was! She was determined that her John was going to enter the teaching profession, one way or another! We were so glad that we had already repaid Val's aunt's loan to us, so we did at least have the proverbial 'roof over our heads'. How we would pay the rates, electricity, gas and phone bills was another matter. In the end, long before 1967 arrived, we had settled the matter. We would go for it, whatever the difficulties. Our love would see us through! My darling wife was so supportive and optimistic about our future life together that I knew it would work; we would make it work, together.

Looking back now, I was so lucky all those years ago that we had such a deep love to see us through these times. Without that and the practical and emotional support from Val, I would never have achieved what was a long and successful career in teaching and education. It also became the foundation stone for another fifty-two years of a very happy marriage!

On reflection, there are some things that I should have covered earlier in this book. It is remiss of me. Understandably, I have concentrated mainly on events in chronological order at the start of our love story. As a result, I may have deprived the reader of some relevant information which is useful in understanding much of the unfolding story. This concerns the situation in Val's home throughout her childhood and early teens. Also, the events that developed her lifelong love of music and her early experiences in employment.

Sadly, Val grew up in a very unhappy home environment. Her father was a violent man and a bully. This violence and dominating nature was mainly directed at her mother, his wife. As a little girl, Val witnessed fights, violence, many arguments and unhappiness that no child should experience. In addition, she was subject to physical abuse herself. As she grew older, she naturally tried to intervene to protect her mother from physical assault, thereby incurring more violence towards herself. When she became a teenager and was able to protect herself from physical abuse, the violence became verbal, as she tried to act as a peacemaker between her parents.

This unhappy situation is all too familiar in many homes even today, where a wife or children are subject to violence behind closed doors, and are often in fear of their lives. In the years when Val was growing up, it was simply kept secret and there were no organisations to turn to for help.

Val loved her mother and did her best to protect her and comfort her as she grew up. When she was older, she tried to persuade her mother to take action, to leave and consider divorce. That did not happen.

Val's mother had a talent for music. She was an accomplished pianist, self-taught; she could play 'by ear' and could not read music. Although in an unhappy marriage, she found great comfort in music and she wanted her only daughter to acquire a love of music too. The family were not poor in financial terms and my future mother-in-law took positive action when Val was a young teenager. She arranged and paid for Val to have professional music lessons on a regular weekly basis. This resulted in Val learning to play the piano and to read music. A little while later, while still in her teens, she also had some professional singing lessons. My future wife was to acquire a love of music and a talent that would last a lifetime.

This love of music was to influence Val's first venture into the world of employment. She worked briefly, part time, at an estate agent's, where she learned to type. Then she got a job in a music shop. This was Moons Ltd. in Exeter's high street. The shop concentrated on classical music, although it did sell 'pop' records. It was also the agency for the ticket sales of orchestral concerts. Val loved working in this environment and she learned a lot. She was surrounded by kind, well-educated staff who looked after her, treated her well and loved her. Something she was not used to in her home. After a few years of happy employment where she loved her work, her colleagues and the opportunity to extend her musical education by attending orchestral concerts, it was all to change. A fateful change too, which was to affect not only Val's life but mine as well.

Val's mother was the catalyst for her change of jobs, somewhat against her will. She kept telling Val that she wasn't earning enough at Moons. Val herself didn't complain about her wages because she was happy in her work. After we were married, she told me what had happened. It seems that Currys, who had a large shop further up the high street, had decided to cash in on the then booming record sales market. They intended to open a new modern record department in the basement of their store, and they wanted to appoint someone to set it all up and manage it. Val's mother saw the large advertisement for this job and thought that Val would be ideal for the post. She was also, I'm sure, influenced by the fact that the salary was more than five times Val's current wages at Moons!

What was remarkable was what happened next. Her mother put in an application on Val's behalf, not telling her until an invitation for an interview at Currys came through the post! Val was understandably unhappy, even quite angry, but she attended the interview and got the job. It is little wonder that she got the job really. She was, I understand, immaculately dressed, if a little conservatively, for the interview. More importantly, she was the only candidate who knew her Beethoven from her Grieg. The envisaged new record department for Currys had to have a specialist classical section, according to the director and manager doing the interviewing, and that was Val's forte.

So Val moved to Currys Ltd. and created the record department there from scratch, and it was a great success. The significance of this will not be lost on the reader, I feel sure. It is ironic that Val's mother, who later so opposed our marriage, was herself instrumental in our first meeting. She was the direct cause of Val's move from Moons to Currys. It was in the basement record department at Currys' high street shop that a young RAF chap, called John, met and fell in love with Valerie Brockley!

Moving on in time, after we were married, Val left Currys when she joined me in Singapore to live as an RAF wife. As the reader will have discovered, she did not need to get a job in Singapore. On our return to the UK, she found her employment with WHSmith in Exeter. With her experience in record sales, this was easy for her, and initially she worked in Smith's record department. Later, she moved to helping out in their larger bookselling section. Her career moved from music and records to books, which she loved. Subsequent employment followed in bookselling, including Pitts, Fagins, Dillons and finally Waterstones bookshops, both full and part time. She was to be very lucky and happy in her working life, which embraced her two great loves: music and literature.

Among the treasured mementoes of Val that I have here are two well-thumbed large books; one is a bookseller's catalogue, the other a remarkable book which lists music composers and their works. Both are very useful to me in solving crosswords and quizzes! I also still have her piano, which sadly sits gathering dust in its current location at the back of my garage!

Chapter 5

On Our Travels – The Early Years

Val was a very intelligent lady. When I met her, she was already very well read, with her lifetime love of music and literature firmly established. Her delight in books and reading had been an escape for her during her very troubled childhood. She told me how she would get away from the rows and unhappy scenes in her home by going to her bedroom with a book. She would read everything she could get her hands on, and by her early teens she was already familiar with classic literature as well as lighter romantic fiction. As a young girl, she would read in bed every night, often well into the early hours. She told me how she would deceive her mother into thinking she was asleep, when secretly still reading. She was aided in this deception because her house at that time had gas lighting and therefore her mother didn't hear her switch the lights on and off! As she grew older, she joined the local library and she would borrow books regularly, both fiction and non-fiction, and poetry. Her active young mind was eager for knowledge and this was now freely available to her. As a result, Val not only had an increased thirst for knowledge but also a growing desire to travel. She wanted to see some of the world and more of her own country; things she had read about.

As already mentioned elsewhere, my secret vow was to make Val's dreams come true. If I could help her achieve what she wanted in life, whatever it was, I would do it. My aim was to make her happy and I was pleased when I was able to do so. Before we met, Val's experience of travel was limited to some journeys to Portsmouth and London, thanks to the kindness of a lady teacher who had befriended her as a teenager. I was determined to change things for Val. Already well travelled myself thanks to RAF service, in 1958, we began our travels together as a married couple.

As you will now know, when we married on 26th October 1957, we had a two-day honeymoon in Taunton. I had promised Val that we would make up for this as soon as possible. Still being a member of the Forces, I had to arrange the necessary leave, and planning holidays, let alone a belated honeymoon, was difficult. In 1958, however, Val and I managed to have our long-delayed and longed-for honeymoon. We travelled to Edinburgh by rail, first class, via London. The journey was good and Val was so excited. Travelling first class in those days was quite something; it meant being absolutely spoilt on the journey, with liveried attendants bringing coffees and afternoon tea and cakes. The trip from King's Cross on the *Flying Scotsman* train was fast and a superb start to the honeymoon. Arriving at Edinburgh Waverly Station, we continued the special occasion in style with a taxi ride to our accommodation, a large guest house in the Morningside suburb of Edinburgh. There we were greeted as 'honeymooners', thanks to my earlier secret arrangements, by the owner, Mr Sidor, and his wife. Originally Mr Sidorsky, he was a Polish ex-fighter pilot in World War II who married a Scot and set up his guest house business. The couple were extremely kind to us throughout the ten-day stay. They gave us special attention, advised us on sightseeing, and pampered us throughout. Val and I had a wonderful late honeymoon as a result. We saw the sights of Edinburgh, walked in the surrounding hills, visited national museums and art galleries, and we were very, very happy and in love. This was the first time I had used my 8mm cine camera, taking pictures of Val in Scotland. I have been able to watch some rather distorted shots from these first films, which I've managed to resurrect on DVDs since Val's death.

Many times over the sixty-one years of our marriage, the late Edinburgh trip, the delayed honeymoon, has been recalled with great fondness by both of us. I am pleased to say that it was just the start of our happy travels together over many years.

During my remaining years on RAF service, I was able to arrange leave at convenient times so that I could take my darling Val to see more of the world. We also made several weekend trips to London to see shows, staying for a night or two. Val's love of music often governed her selection of shows. I always tried to let her choose; I was determined that her dreams would be fulfilled, not mine. To see her happy was enough for me, as she was when we saw *West Side Story* in London with the original Broadway cast. Val's favourite popular singer was Johnny Mathis; I have fond memories of listening to his dulcet tones singing love songs during our courting days and early years of marriage. To please Val, we also travelled to see Mathis in live shows on five separate occasions, in London, Birmingham and Bristol. To honour my darling wife, I insisted on *The Twelfth of Never* by Mathis being played at the end of her funeral service in February 2019.

Our first trip overseas on holiday as a couple was to Paris in 1959. Again, Val was in her element. She loved every minute of it; she loved being treated as a 'lady' and she revelled in the art, the history and the sights of romantic Paris. Many years later, Val told me how she felt so special when a uniformed doorman at the Hotel Francia gave her an umbrella and ushered us out into a rainy Parisian evening. We were staying in an upmarket hotel in the centre of Paris; we had travelled first class on the boat train from London and no expense was spared to make the holiday memorable, for Val. That first overseas trip for Val certainly held a special place in her memories and was often talked about down the decades of our marriage.

Those years when I was still in the RAF allowed us to have other holidays, usually in Europe. Val had quickly got used to holidaying abroad and she was eager to see some of the things and places that she had read about and even dreamt about. Seaside holidays in Belgium and France were followed by guided-tour trips to the World War I battlefields and the Normandy beaches of World War II at Arromanches in France. Val was very caring and sentimental about the 'war-trip' holidays; she always told me that it moved her greatly thinking of the many who had died in Europe in the two world wars. One particularly significant holiday comes to mind during this period: our first journey together to Austria.

Once again, Val's love of music influenced this choice of venue. We had been to see the film *The Sound of Music*, and Val often mentioned the fact that Salzburg had a famous music festival. Her favourite conductor, Herbert V. Karajan, usually performed there and, of course, it was the birthplace of Mozart! So we booked a holiday at the most prestigious hotel in the ski resort of Kitzbühel, reasonably close to Salzburg. We were able to climb mountains and enjoy the Tyrol but also visit Salzburg and see the birthplace of Mozart and places where *The Sound of Music* was filmed. I also took some 8mm movie cine film on the Austrian holiday. Recently, I have been able to watch my DVD edition with Val wandering up the Kitzbüheler Horn Mountain and writing postcards outside, in the garden of the hotel, this more than fifty years later. Quite wonderful!

We visited France and Belgium quite a few times in those early years of our marriage. In those days, one did not have the convenience of low-cost flights by easyJet! We did what most people did. We travelled by sea and train. An important part of my vow to fulfil Val's dreams and make her life happy, we always travelled first class on trains and where available on boats too. An added delight for Val was the fact that she spoke French well, and in the French-speaking countries we often visited at this time, she was able to use her language skills a lot. My own linguistic skills did cover French of a schoolboy variety, but Val's French accent was superb and much better than mine! Throughout our long marriage, Val would tease me over this. She had a lovely singing voice and, of course, she had professional music training. She would tease me by suddenly bursting into song and singing the whole of the French National Anthem in French, all the verses and chorus with an accent that Édith Piaf would have been proud of! This habit of enjoying singing *The Marseillaise* was to stay with Val all through her eighty-plus years. You will be reminded of this near the end of this book, when my darling Val was also near her end.

All our early holidays were not a complete success. Ever since we watched the film *Zorba the Greek* in a cinema, Val had wanted to visit Greece. A few months after my return from Singapore on a stretcher, I was gradually regaining my health, and my thoughts turned to making Val's latest travel dream come true. A trip to Greece. I invested a considerable sum on an upmarket holiday. Flights were with the then very popular Laker Airways and I rented a villa on what was then a little-known Greek island, Symi. "Unspoilt by tourists, very natural, live as the Greeks do," they said. We flew to Rhodes.

After a nightmare trip across a choppy sea on a rather small ancient steamer from Rhodes, I enquired about the location of the Villa Michaelaria. "Eet is up there," a lovely young lady informed us, pointing to a distant mountain. "We go up the steps." Only I could have chosen an island where we had to climb more than 700 steps and follow a mountain track which even gave the local donkeys trouble! Val didn't wish to speak to me on our arrival at the villa. In fact, she was in no physical state to do so. Over the next two weeks, there were several new experiences for us on our travels.

One day, Greek hospitality proved too much for me. I consumed vast amounts of the local Metaxa brandy while making the acquaintance of some local people, with the result that I was violently sick for two days! On another occasion, while we were having dinner, the peace was disturbed by an earthquake! The real gem of this holiday was reserved for our return journey, however. The ancient steamer that had brought us to the island was out of action. So in order to catch our plane at Rhodes, the tour operator chartered a small fishing boat. We were to rendezvous with our replacement steamer literally in mid-ocean. The closest we have ever come to being lost at sea was while we were trying to clamber up the side of a moving ship in a choppy sea with suitcases but without the aid of a ladder! Our fellow passengers were all very pale and shaken, with more than one elderly person close to a complete fit or breakdown. In spite of it all, it must be said that Greek hospitality was superb, their country beautiful and their friendliness out of this world. It was certainly a holiday to remember and we often talked about our adventure in Greece many times during our long marriage. It is telling that Val and I did not visit Greece again, ever!

This chapter must include the longest holiday journey we ever made together: six weeks at sea! While we were living in Singapore, our daily paper was the *Straits Times*, the English-language paper, long established in the region. One page of the newspaper that we enjoyed reading was the Shipping Section in its business section. I frequently brought Val's attention to a Scottish shipping line's entries, the Ben Line of Leith, the port of Edinburgh. These showed that Ben Line regularly plied its trade between the UK and the Far East. One day, I noticed something very interesting. Ben Line ships, although predominantly cargo vessels, often carried a limited number of passengers.

An idea came together gradually over a period of weeks; why not consider returning to the UK at the end of my tour by sea? It would be quite an adventure and the real journey of a lifetime. Val was keen on the idea, so I began to make some enquiries about the viability for us as a couple. I had to make sure that it was okay with the RAF; that I would have enough weeks of leave and that we could afford it! Of course, we could travel back to the UK in less than two days with the RAF, by air. This would not cost us anything and I would then have several weeks' leave in the UK to follow. We thought about it for some weeks. After all, the cost of such a sea trip would be enough to refurnish our small cottage in Exeter and still leave some money as savings. However, our excitement mounted, the more we thought about it. We decided to take the plunge and go for it. In the back of my mind, I saw this as another step in giving Val an exciting and better life; to make more good memories for her to hold on to in the future; to make our love and marriage special.

I contacted the shipping office in Singapore City; we looked at sailing dates and we planned as much as we could. We were both thrilled when we were able to eventually book the passage. We were to sail on the 10,000-ton plus Ben Line *SS Benloyal* early in 1966, along with eight other passengers and a large cargo of freight. The trip back to England would take six weeks and we would be sailing halfway around the world!

We were busy in the weeks before our embarkation. We were ostensibly travelling as civilians and the RAF gave me strict orders on what I could and could not do. All RAF items, including every bit of my uniform, had to be packed and crated to go back to the UK separately via the RAF. I had to strictly adhere to other things; not to talk about the RAF at any time; to say simply that I was 'on Government Service'. This was understandable at this time in 1966, as we would be passing through several warzones, and the Cold War was still on everyone's mind. This was particularly true of the Middle East, in Aden, and even in parts of Malaya and Indonesia. We would, therefore, be really travelling somewhat incognito, civilian clothes at all times.

The great day arrived at last and we set off for the docks in Singapore with some good friends, in taxis. A couple of Welsh friends, Ken and Mary Evans, and their two young children were with us to wish us *bon voyage*. They were equally excited when we were able to take them on board the *Benloyal* and show them around our suite of accommodation. We had our own bathroom, lounge and bedroom in the suite, and even a Malay steward of our own! Val and I felt like royals, and we were convinced that we had made the right decision. The Evans family enjoyed tea and cakes in our suite, courtesy of our steward on board, before they reluctantly left the ship with many hugs and tears. We were waved off from the dockside and began our great sea adventure.

We met the other passengers later at dinner while still steaming in the Straits of Johor. The most distinguished passenger was the retiring Chief of the Malayan Police Service, who had flown down from Kuala Lumpur to join the *Benloyal*. He was with his wife and security man. Another passenger was a self-made businessman, a bachelor called Fred Pashley. He was on a world cruise and he had joined the *Benloyal* after a few weeks in Hong Kong. There was an older lady, I recall, a widow, who had spent a lifetime on a tea plantation in Malaya, and several older couples who had been civil servants in the Foreign Office. Val and I were easily the youngest passengers on board, so it is not surprising that we spent most of our time on the ship to ourselves. We both thought of it as a late second honeymoon and behaved accordingly! Watching the flying fishes from the rails as we crossed the Indian Ocean, arms around one another, comes to mind!

Having enjoyed more than two years living together as a couple for the first time, this journey back to the UK, by sea, was the icing on the cake! We had enjoyed so much of the previous two years together; this was a wonderful opportunity to build on and to further strengthen our marriage. We had already been used to a life of some luxury in Singapore, so we simply embraced the chance to have more experiences on the trip home. We were very happy.

The *Benloyal* sailed up the coast of Malaya and docked in Penang, an island state of the Federation of Malaya. The ship had to load a large cargo of freight there and this meant that there was an overnight stay, meaning Val and I could go ashore and explore Penang. We had offers to join other passengers on a sightseeing tour of the city, George Town, and the countryside, but luckily we decided to go our own way. As a result, we had a great first visit to Penang. We rode in rickshaws through crowded streets, taking in the sights, the colours and the spicy smells; we shopped briefly, bargaining like the locals for small trinkets and souvenirs; we visited a sacred temple dedicated to turtles; and then, after a meal, we abandoned travel by rickshaw for a large taxi. The taxi took us outside the city of Penang and deep into the countryside, down a winding road with thick Malayan jungle on both sides. The taxi driver stopped at the side of the road and asked us what we would like to do. After some discussion and a little haggling over prices, all conducted in a cheerful and friendly manner, we asked the delighted Malayan driver to take us to the nearest beach. He happily agreed and told us that he would leave us alone 'like lovers' for an hour and collect us later!

Val and I found ourselves on a beautiful beach, with pristine white sand, palm trees with coconuts, a lovely calm blue sea and a sunny sky. There was not a soul to be seen anywhere (apart from the taxi driver, who was already asleep in his car!), not even footprints on the hot sand. Paradise! It was just like a scene from a film. We slipped off our sandals, I took Val's hand and we slowly walked along the hot white sand, marvelling at the sheer beauty of it all. This was the year 1966, after all. There were no buildings to be seen; simply a mile or so of white beach, palm trees, the occasional chattering of monkeys in the trees, birds with wonderful colouring and a gently lapping blue sea. There were no snack bars, no sunbathers, no people! It was Val and I alone together in a tropical paradise! We loved it. We stopped to hug one another and to kiss from time to time and we paddled at the water's edge, vowing our love for one another in whispered words. Unfortunately, the hour went by all too quickly and our cheerful taxi driver was waving to us once again. We never forgot Penang throughout our sixty-one years of marriage, and I can still rekindle those memories in an instant, with considerable joy and pleasure, today.

When the taxi pulled up at the *Benloyal* berthed in the docks, she was still a hive of activity; cranes working overtime and what seemed like an army of labourers teeming around the ship, directed by the ship's officers and crew. Over dinner that evening, on board, we were given a detailed account of what was happening. It seemed that there was always a tight time schedule when the ship was berthed and taking on its cargo, hence the gangs of local workers and their gang leaders working everywhere. We were told that Singapore and Penang were very popular ports with the Ben Line crews.

The following morning, Val and I strolled up onto the deck, after a very nice breakfast, to quite a shock for us! From the dull throb of the engines in the early hours, we knew the ship had set sail, but as we looked out over the rails, all we saw was sea, everywhere! We were steaming well out into the Indian Ocean, the sun was beating down and we knew we were really on our way home. For more than a week we saw nothing but sea, flying fishes and a tropical sun; it was wonderful. The peace was disturbed once or twice by a tropical storm and heavy rain, but most of the time we relaxed on sun loungers on deck, reading and talking to one another. As the youngest couple on board, we were left alone most of the time. Our steward plied us with cold drinks and various refreshments, attending to our every need!

During this crossing of the Indian Ocean, Val and I began to think and talk about our future life together. We discussed all the possibilities and it turned out to be a very useful exercise. The idea for me to give up my RAF career came to a head at this time, and plans for my teaching career started to take shape. We both agreed that we wanted a life that ensured we would be together all the time. Our years in Singapore had convinced the two of us that it would work and be the best thing for our marriage.

The next port of call for the *Benloyal* was the port of Aden. Today, the Republic of Yemen. Unfortunately, Aden was then in the early throes of its 'war of independence' against British rule. As a result, we were not allowed to go ashore there on British military orders. We could only view Aden from the safety of the ship. I had been to Aden many times before on RAF flights, so I was able to give Val a brief description of its charms, or rather lack of them! I had never liked the place; it was full of flies, disease and slums. Not a great legacy of British rule, I'm afraid, so I spent some time giving my thoughts on the place to Val. I encouraged her to concentrate on the next part of our journey home: the Red Sea, the Egyptian ports and the Suez Canal.

Sailing the full length of the Red Sea was quite an experience, and we constantly looked at a large atlas to find out where exactly we were each day. Eventually, when we were close to the Suez area, I reminded Val that although we could only see desert, sun and not much else on both sides of the ship, in one direction was the Egyptian resort of Sharm el-Sheikh, and not so far away was the Israeli resort of Eilat. My mention of Israel did spark something in Val. She was unusually excited when she said, "That's the Holy Land. I want to go there one day." How significant those words turned out to be! Some years later, we were to go to the Holy Land on holiday for the first of five visits we made there. It was to become a very special place for both of us, particularly for Val.

After a few more days sailing, I pointed out to Val exactly where we were on the map. We had arrived in the Strait of Gubal, where the Red Sea forked. To our left was the Gulf of Suez, leading to Port Taufiq and the entrance to the Suez Canal; to the right was the Gulf of Aqaba leading to Aqaba itself in Jordan and the developing Israeli port of Eliat. She was really excited for several days, as she realised where we were in the world at that precise time. I am sure it was the close proximity of Jordan and Israel that really intrigued her. She had read about Lawrence of Arabia, Aqaba and, of course, the Holy Land of Israel, and it fascinated her. The ship was moving slowly now as it made its way up the Gulf of Suez, so we had ample time to take in the scenery. The scenery in reality was a burning sun beating down all of the time, and desert everywhere; the Eastern Desert of Egypt on one side and Sinai on the other. As the *Benloyal* made its way up the Gulf of Suez, we saw our first camels! A slowly moving caravan of camels could be seen alongside the water, and Val had an excellent view of them through binoculars borrowed from a ship's officer. We were able to see many more later. The ship had to anchor in Port Taufiq and wait a day or so for other ships to join it in order to make up a convoy to pass through the Suez Canal. After the Egyptian pilots boarded, we eventually set off up the Canal.

This was another new experience for us. We were amazed at how narrow it was and how ships passed each other en route. There was also now much more to see. Instead of just desert and the odd palm tree, we saw some people, donkeys and camels! We were now moving through the British-controlled Suez Canal Zone, so there were small relics of the British influence, little townships, oases and Bedouin camps.

We asked one of the ship's officers if we would be able to go ashore at Port Said when we left the Canal. Unfortunately, we could not. Egypt was not particularly stable or friendly with the UK at that time. However, the officer did assure us that we would be able to buy souvenirs before we sailed into the Mediterranean Sea. He told us that the *Benloyal*'s captain would allow a limited number of Arab pedlars, or 'Bumboat Men' as he called them, to come on board. Closely watched, they would be allowed to sell things to the ship's passengers, staying on the ship's decks for the few miles up to Port Said.

This excited Val and she talked to other passengers about it at dinner that evening. Some of the older passengers had made the Suez trip before and were quite used to this. Val told me that she was going to buy some presents for herself and her family. I didn't know how to respond. Although it was my first trip up the Suez Canal, I had flown into some RAF bases in the region before: Libya, Iraq and the old Suez Canal Zone. I knew what those Arab traders were like. They were certainly not like the vision that Val had of them! I kept quiet, of course. I wanted Val to keep her idealistic view of things; she was so excited that I couldn't bring myself to spoil her dreams.

We both watched these Arab traders arrive. They scrambled up rope ladders with great agility and skill. Each of them had huge containers on their backs containing their wares, and they began to set up their sales pitches along the decks of the *Benloyal*. I made a point of securing our valuables immediately! Having hidden passports, wallets and money about my person, I took Val's hand and we set off to go shopping along the decks of the ship. Val ended up, in spite of my protests, with a miscellany of souvenirs. She learned quickly about the art of bargaining in the Middle-Eastern world. A small handbag offered to her at twenty pounds sterling was eventually bought for two pounds. The so-called leather items were not, of course, real leather but camel hide. Val was to find this out many weeks later in Exeter; the stuffed camels she bought were filled with desert sand which leaked out quite quickly!

Looking back now, the most amusing incident was when Val came to me and complained about one Arab trader. She told me that he kept creeping up to her and whispering to her. He called her 'Mrs Victoria' and was offering to sell her something special. This item was in a small glass bottle and it was very expensive. I could not contain myself and I burst into laughter when she asked me exactly what 'Spanish Fly' was used for!

Val was so innocent that I had to be careful how I explained things to her. Spanish Fly was supposed to be an ancient natural aphrodisiac which would make men particularly sexually potent and virile. It would work wonders for the sex drive, performance and desire in both males and females. I had heard of it but not sampled it, I hasten to add! A super efficient old-world version of modern-day Viagra, I suppose. Listening to me, Val was quite amused at first, but then became rather angry.

"What a cheek," she said. "You don't need that, neither do I!"

I discreetly made myself scarce as she went off to give that Arab a piece of her mind. Needless to say, she came back with another worthless necklace that someone had persuaded her to buy!

While we were anchored in Port Said for a few days, I managed to tell Val a little about Israel. She was fascinated and she even went to the ship's small library to borrow some books so that she could learn some more. I had never been to Israel but Val was intrigued when I told her that Eliat, the Israeli Red Sea port, was where Moses had entered the Promised Land on his flight from Egypt with the Israelites after crossing the Red Sea into Sinai.

The Arab traders soon departed when we docked in Port Said. We watched them leave in a more comfortable way for them, via the ship's gangplank steps. With fellow passengers, we lined the ship's rails and waved them off. They seemed very cheerful and happy; business must have been good for them even without the sale of Spanish Fly to Valerie!

A day later, the *Benloyal* set sail out into the Mediterranean Sea. The weather was wonderful and it suited us because the humidity had dropped and we could enjoy sunbathing in an ideal hot climate. As we steamed across the blue sea, there was only one significant incident. We were the only ship in our part of the Mediterranean at the time, although we had already seen other vessels en route. There was suddenly a commotion on deck. Val and I quickly got up from our sun loungers to investigate. We joined some other passengers at the rails to see what was going on. Suddenly we saw a submarine which was surfacing very close to the *Benloyal*. It was no more than one hundred metres or so from our starboard side. The way that this large grey shape appeared from beneath the water, silently and mysteriously, like the Loch Ness Monster, was quite surreal and something we had never experienced before.

One of the ship's young officers with binoculars calmly informed us that it was a Russian submarine. I had my own opinion and views, naturally. As the grey submarine settled on the surface and began to silently and rapidly move away from our ship, I told Val that I thought they were 'playing games' with us; that they had deliberately closed in on the *Benloyal* in order to surprise us. It certainly scared me! The fact that there had been nothing but the blue sea one minute and then this rather ominous shape of a large submarine very close to us was quite frightening. The incident was still being discussed around our dinner table that evening. We learned from the ship's senior officer that they were quite used to it. Evidently, the Mediterranean was constantly 'policed' by both Russia and the US, and the Royal Navy, at that time. My RAF experience did allow me some small consolation in knowing that a lot of ships and submarines would have been aware of what was happening that day. The Russian sub would have been plotted and shown up on many radar screens. The US Navy and the RN would have known exactly where the Russian warship was! It probably brought a smile to many a Russian submariner that day, and it certainly remains clear in my memory.

We continued on an uneventful trip home after that day, sailing via Gibraltar back to the UK. The next excitement came as we entered the Thames to begin our slow progress up to London. We were delighted when we eventually entered the King George V Dock in London, and began to pack our cases in our suite on the ship. The *Benloyal* had been our home for six weeks, and we had enjoyed a quite outstanding experience on the voyage from Singapore.

We had cabled our families from the ship and given them times, dates and some details of our arrival in

London. What we did not know was that we would be greeted at the dockside by two of Val's family. Her Aunt Beatrice and Uncle Jim had driven up to London to welcome us home. This was the aunt who had lent us the money to buy our little cottage in Exeter. The same kind lady who had therefore been instrumental in allowing us to get married in 1957. It was a lovely surprise for us, although tinged with sadness when we found out the news that Val's mother had been diagnosed with motor neurone disease and could not travel with her sister to London. We entertained Val's aunt and uncle with afternoon tea in our suite on the ship before disembarking and saying our farewells to passengers and the crew.

Another blessing was that Val's aunt offered to take our cases back with them in the boot of their car. They were having a few days' holiday in London before returning to Exeter and their business there. We were very pleased about that, because that meant Val and I could make our own way home by train without the rather large and heavy cases. We would see them again in a few days' time. We had an excellent journey home to Exeter via taxi to Paddington Station and train.

Val and I were always excited when we began to plan our holidays for a coming year. 1982 was an extra special year for us because on the 26th of October 1982 we would reach our Silver Wedding. Twenty-five years was quite a milestone and something special for us to look forward to. We decided to have UK holidays in the spring, perhaps Scotland or Cornwall. That left us to consider October and the special one.

A year or two earlier in Exeter, we had met a lovely couple from Canada by chance. Fred and Ruby Downey had been touring the UK on a pilgrimage of sorts because Fred had been stationed in England as a very young soldier in the Canadian Army. He was a D-Day veteran, and he was revisiting the UK to rekindle his memories of World War II. We struck up an instantly mutual friendship which blossomed over time. Fred and Ruby stayed at our house in Exeter for a week. Val lavished attention on them and showed her excellent culinary skills to great effect! We wined and dined them, took them out for meals and took them on visits to Torquay and other tourist locations in Devon. They appreciated it and for a year or two, Val continued to correspond with them after they had returned to Toronto where they lived.

Naturally, they wanted to reciprocate our hospitality and friendship, urging us to visit them in Canada whenever we could. A plan began to take shape when we were thinking about our silver wedding. Why not try to make that long-awaited trip to Canada in October? We started to make plans early in 1982.

It will be evident to the reader from other chapters that Val valued and cherished her friendships. She was a lovely, natural person who cared. At this time, she also maintained several friendships with former colleagues of hers in the bookselling business. One of these was Phyllis Chudley and her husband, Fred. Phyllis had worked with Val at WHSmith for many years, and they often met for coffee and a chat in Exeter. They got on well, although Phyl was much older than Val. They had a mutual interest in all things literary, the royal family and visits to historical sites. They often went to London together by train for a day to go to an exhibition or for some occasion. They would really live it up by visiting Harrods, Fortnum & Mason, Selfridges and the like! They would take afternoon tea at the Dorchester or the Ritz on occasion, just to prove that they could do it. Phyl had spent many years working and living in London, so Val was grateful for her skills when travelling around the capital.

When this good friend of Val's heard that we were planning to visit Toronto for our silver wedding, she was overjoyed. She told us that her younger brother, John Bradbury, had emigrated to Canada years before, married a local Canadian girl called Isabel and lived with his wife and two children in Toronto. Never backward in giving the younger Val orders, she told us that we had to visit them in October on our holiday. So now we had extra reasons to visit Canada. I then conjured up another treat for Val by suggesting that on our anniversary day, 26th October, I would take her to Niagara Falls.

The year flashed by and all our plans were in place for our trip to Canada. Inevitably, things go wrong. There are always unforeseen problems. Two things went wrong at this time. Firstly, on our way to Heathrow for our Air Canada flight to Toronto, I lost a suitcase! We did something we rarely did and took a coach to travel to Heathrow instead of the trusted train. The coach stopped first at Gatwick, where some passengers got off. Proceeding to Heathrow, I happily collected my main suitcase from the coach, only to discover that it wasn't my case. It was identical to mine, same colour and size; however, the label named someone going from Gatwick to Kenya! In a considerable state of panic, I had to leave Val at Heathrow with our small luggage and flag down a taxi with instructions to 'follow that coach' which was on its way to Victoria Coach Station.

To be fair, the staff and the London cabbie were first class in the help they offered. Eventually, after many phone calls and lots of anxiety, another coach delivered my case to me at Heathrow in exchange for the Kenya-bound case. Val and I made the book-in time for our flight by just twenty minutes! For probably the first time in our twenty-five-year marriage, Val was really glaring at me and reluctant to speak to me. What a start to our silver wedding celebration!

"Why didn't you check it more carefully?" and similar questions were all I got from Val until we were airborne. I decided that I would not try to repair the damage immediately so I said nothing until we were an hour or so into the flight, when I tentatively reached for her hand, and I was very relieved to get a reassuring squeeze in return. After some in-flight meals and helped by several Courvoisier brandy and dries, Val's favourite tipple, things improved rapidly. I at last began to think that this holiday was going to be just as special as we had planned it to be.

On landing in the evening at Toronto International Airport, we nervously made our way through the crowds to look for a taxi. Suddenly Val came to a standstill and told me to look over at the crowds of people awaiting passengers. There, holding up a large homemade sign saying '*Mr & Mrs Salmon*', was a smartly suited man and two teenage children. That was how we first met John Bradbury and his children, Sarah and Iain. We quickly discovered that Val's friend, Phyl Chudley, John's older sister, had telephoned from Chard Road in Exeter during the day and virtually ordered him to meet us at the airport! We were delighted.

Although we had an invitation to stay with Fred and Ruby Downey at their bungalow, we felt it better to arrange some accommodation at a hotel for ourselves for a few days and to look up Fred and Ruby when we were in Canada. Val thought it would be unfair to simply arrive at the older couple's front door looking to stay for a few days.

That brings me to the second thing that I got wrong on the silver wedding trip! I had booked a medium standard hotel close to Lake Ontario; remember, this was long before online booking facilities! What I did not know was that the hotel I had booked was in a particular area, well known to the locals. The hotel turned out to be in the middle of a group of hotels favoured by rich Canadians, mainly businessmen, when with their mistresses or lady friends. In other words, Val and I were staying in Toronto's posh but definitely 'Red Light' district! At least it was the upmarket end of those hotels, but Val was not particularly amused when she found out my blunder. Luckily, I had only booked the hotel for a few nights and for most of our holiday we were with Fred and Ruby in Willowdale, and John and Isabel and their children in Don Mills, the upmarket suburbs of Toronto.

As we left the airport chatting excitedly to our new friends, particularly the children, who were excited at meeting their Auntie Phyl's friends from England, we came to a really huge Chrysler car, and John Bradbury took our cases and stowed them in its cavernous boot. We really knew then that we were in North America, where everything seems to be big, really big. John was a lecturer at Toronto University and they lived in the richest area of Toronto so naturally he would have a very large limousine!

We were whisked off in the night and soon arrived at our lakeside hotel, at that time quite unaware of the 'Red Light' connection, thank goodness. We thanked our new friends and the children for all their kindness and took their phone numbers, address, and so on, promising to get in touch the following day. We had arrived at last, what a day! John Bradbury had also given us detailed instructions on how to use the Toronto Subway system, as there was a station close to the hotel. What a superb means of transport that proved to be throughout our holiday. It was fast, efficient and immaculately clean. It puts London and the Paris Metro to shame. So our special silver wedding holiday got off to an eventful start in more ways than one, but it turned out to be a truly memorable ten days for Val and I.

Throughout the holiday, we were looked after so well by the two couples. We dined superbly at Fred and Ruby's bungalow in Willowdale. As they were much older than us, we would not let them show us the sights as they offered to do; but we spent many enjoyable hours with them. We did our own sightseeing in the first few days in Toronto, taking in the CN Tower and other landmarks. We would start each day with a good and very large

Canadian breakfast at a restaurant, having journeyed in on the Subway from our lakeside hotel. We saw Wells Fargo trucks and Mounties everywhere in the spotlessly clean centre of Toronto.

We had contacted the Bradburys by phone on our first day in Canada and we had arranged to meet up later in the week. So for a few days we were alone together, exploring the fantastic city of Toronto. Our visit to the tallest building, the CN Tower, was particularly memorable. Hand in hand like very young lovers, we went up in the lift and dined in the restaurant, with awesome views over the city. The following day was our anniversary day, 26th October. Very excited, we set off on the Subway early in the morning for the main rail station. It went like clockwork! We boarded a huge long Amtrak train bound for New York via Hamilton and Niagara. Coffees and waffles drenched in maple syrup were consumed on the train. We got off the train at Niagara Station. It was a little disappointing to see how commercialised Niagara was to our eyes. I was, however, secretly pleased that Val declined my offer for me to sign up in one of the many chapels and churches that offered instant 'Repeat Your Marriage Vows Services'! Not for us, I'm pleased to say. The day was still very special, although we did not go out in a boat on the Falls. We were blissfully happy when we persuaded another visiting couple to take a photo of us together by the Falls.

After a day to remember, good food and lots to see and talk about, we eventually took the evening train back to Toronto. We clung to each other on the train going back and on the Subway. Safely back in our hotel, we had a truly great night in bed, our lovemaking reflecting our day as we remembered our first night as a married couple twenty-five years before at the Rose Inn in Taunton.

The following day, we used the Subway again to go into Toronto. Having been welcomed at our favourite restaurant in the city centre and devouring another huge breakfast, we set off for the suburbs of Don Mills to look up the Bradbury family. We had been surprised by one thing as we went through Toronto; the fact that approaching Halloween on the 31st of October, the city centre was full of decorations, witches, pumpkins, ghouls and ghosts and the like. We hadn't been aware that Halloween was so big in North America. Val and I went into a large bank to change some travellers' cheques and the whole bank was decorated in a Halloween theme. The staff were all in professionally made costumes as witches, wizards, ghosts and ghouls! It was a bit scary at first but certainly unique and quite a surprise to us.

Later, when we were sipping drinks in the Bradburys' large lounge, John and Isabel told us that Canadians 'do' Halloween properly just like they do in the USA! Their teenage children, Sarah and Iain, were keen to show us their Halloween costumes and already prepared pumpkins and their house decorations. The children were obviously very excited about it all and eager for the 31st to come!

We were royally entertained and looked after at the Bradburys' home. They treated us magnificently throughout our few days with them with wonderful hospitality. They wined and dined us like royals and took us by car to see other parts of Ontario, and we did enjoy a Halloween the like of which we had never experienced before or since. One day, they took us to Black Creek Village, which was quite out of this world for us. To meet real Native Americans and see some wonderful old crafts in action and artefacts from a bygone age made it another day to remember.

Like Val and I, the Bradbury family loved animals, in particular cats. They had a large and rather ancient cat called Ginger and a small kitten whom Ginger tolerated! How Ginger became their pet was quite a story. It seems that John, Isabel and the two children were out in a forest area, walking carefully to avoid the possibility of meeting up with a large black bear or other forest creatures. It was winter and very cold. There was snow everywhere; they suddenly heard a plaintive animal's cry, and the children insisted their parents investigate the source. They discovered to their horror that a ginger cat was in great distress close to a very large tree. It turned out that its legs were frozen to the tree and part of its body also. How this happened they did not know, but a freak accident of nature perhaps, and the cat would have either starved to death or possibly been eaten by another animal, if left there. They had to summon help from the Animal Rescue Service and a vet, but the cat was rescued and recovered from its ordeal. As no one claimed ownership, Iain and Sarah insisted he become their pet. So Ginger spent his last few years in the lap of luxury, and for a few days, he also experienced Val's and John's laps and lots of loving and stroking, for which he rewarded us with deep purrs!

Having enjoyed a wonderful few days, including Halloween, with the Bradbury family and their cats, we said our reluctant farewells to them. We had promised Fred and Ruby Downey that we would spend our last day in Canada with them at their bungalow in the suburb of Willowdale. We were due to fly out that evening and Fred insisted on driving us to the airport. Ruby had arranged a farewell dinner for us and during that day we met their daughter for the first time. We were really treated like important and distinguished guests by both our host families in Toronto, and this added to the special occasion of our anniversary. We had combined a few days on our own, including The Day at Niagara, with some great days with two lovely families who certainly knew how to welcome guests with superb hospitality.

On the evening of our departure, after a really splendid meal with Ruby and Fred, we had two hours to go before we were due to set off for the airport. Fred then decided that we should all have a few drinks to celebrate our anniversary and the holiday. If only Val and I had known what Fred's idea of 'a few drinks' was! He began mixing cocktails like someone out of a film, and we discovered that he liked gin with a little bitters. They insisted on filling our glasses regularly and we found ourselves consuming cocktails and spirits of all kinds, together with a variety of nuts, snacks and salad items. I distinctly remember staggering out to Fred's large Buick limousine with our cases, and I initially saw two identical Buicks there! There was only one!

I didn't even think about Fred's ability to drive us safely to the airport. Wisely, his wife, Ruby, decided to stay at home; she said her goodbyes at her bungalow. I do recall Fred muttering something about how 'this car can drive itself to Toronto International' during the journey! I squeezed Val's hand in the back of the car and hoped that we wouldn't feel sick. Somehow, eventually, we got to the airport on time. I do now realise that Fred was a regular drinker in a social sense, unlike Val and I, or possibly he had 'doctored' his own drinks during the evening, reducing the alcohol levels. We said our farewells and boarded our Air Canada flight to Heathrow. Truth be told, we didn't really remember much about the eight-and-a- half-hour flight to London.

In a strange way, the drinking session was a blessing, as we both slept soundly on the flight. We did consume lots of coffee before we got to Heathrow, after declining the proffered cooked breakfast meals. We both had considerable hangovers when we travelled back to Exeter by train. We had given up coach travel after our episode with the suitcase ten days before!

Sadly, there is an unhappy postscript to this account of our silver wedding anniversary trip to Canada. Isabel Bradbury, our lovely hostess for much of the holiday, wife of John and mother to Sarah and Iain, died only a few years later at only fifty-two years of age, from breast cancer. She was a lovely lady, a wonderful wife and mother, and the main saviour of Ginger the cat. We kept in touch with John and the two children for many years, including on a visit the three of them made to the UK.

That 1982 trip to Canada for our silver wedding was often recalled by Val and I over the years. We would look at our photo album dedicated to the trip and remember clearly the wonderful hospitality and affection shown to us by the Downeys and the Bradburys of Toronto. In

2018, when Val was in her care home in Teignmouth, a year before she died, I arrived one day to find her staring at the board of photos in her room on the wall facing her bed, and she pointed out the Niagara photos to me, with a broad smile on her face. She never forgot that holiday and our day at Niagara Falls, even at eighty-two years of age with a debilitating illness. We had been forty-six then and very much in love, as always.

Chapter 6

Married and a Schoolteacher

Early in 1967, after twelve years' service in the RAF, I left and became a civilian. Val and I celebrated the occasion with a modest meal out and a glass of wine, no party or meeting up with friends. We were too concerned about the prospects for our future life together in the civilian world. We worried about the financial aspects. We had certainly been comfortably off while I was in the RAF and in secure employment. Now we did not know what the future held for us. Luckily, Val was an excellent and careful housekeeper. Regarding the finances, we owned our own house, and we had discussed things thoroughly. We had plans in place. I was due to start my teacher's course in October 1967 when my local government grant would start. Val arranged to work full time at WHSmith as a bookseller. She was very valuable to that firm because of her musical experience; she could also work in their record department, when needed.

I managed to obtain temporary employment as a civil servant at the Ministry of Pensions & National Insurance Office in Exeter; this was quite a shock for me! The work was not difficult but very boring; the pay was abysmally low and the working environment left much to be desired. How on earth anyone could spend a lifetime working as a civil servant, I will never know! Nevertheless, it helped us at the time. I was able to walk to work from St David's to Pennsylvania Road in Exeter, and we did have the bonus of being able to meet for lunch together on most days. It really was a truly wonderful 'first' for us. Hectic times, I remember. We were both out of breath when we arrived at our little cottage. Luckily, we were both fit, and the rapid walk helped. I would manage a quick hug and kiss as Val fed our cat, Fluffy, and produced our lunch sandwiches, which she had prepared already. Val was marvellous at managing a multi-task situation and still remaining upbeat and cheerful.

This new lifestyle soon became a routine and, although difficult, it strengthened our marriage at a vital time of transition. It is true to say that our love flourished during this time! I had never been able to see Val every day until then. To see her midday as well was great. We couldn't go out for entertainment or meals in the evenings for five days each week. We were both too tired and besides, money was tight. We did, however, make up for it at weekends. We visited parents and family, went to the cinema, had drinks and coffees in town and simply went for walks, holding hands like young lovers do!

When October came, I was quite excited to be embarking on my teacher training. By then, we knew that we would be able to manage financially; we had adapted well to civilian life and we were more in love than ever!

Perhaps it would be appropriate here for me to mention that although the title of this chapter contains the word 'schoolteacher', I do not intend to go into detail about my educational experiences or to chronologically document my career as a teacher. Some of it will come out as a matter of course as the memories of this period of our marriage are covered. To write in detail about my many years in education is impossible here; they would need a book of their own. That's another project for another day!

As usual, Val was great in supporting me during my teacher training. She kept working full time, bringing in valuable funds to add to the government grant. She bought books for me, through Smiths, obtaining a staff discount, and she spent many hours typing up my essays and university work. She even made many of my visual aids for lessons on my teaching practices!

When I started training to be a teacher, I was thirty-one years old and a 'mature' student. I was still undecided whether I should enter the primary or the secondary sector. Luckily, I received some excellent advice from the Exeter University lecturers in Education. As a result, I transferred to a two-year Certificate in Education course which would allow me to teach in both primary and secondary schools. I could therefore defer making this crucial decision. The very good advice also suggested that it was a useful thing to gain teaching experience in both sectors, starting with primary schools and seeing where my strengths and interests lay. In fact, that is exactly what happened over subsequent years. During my career in education, I taught in rural and urban primary schools, some secondary grammar and comprehensive schools, even briefly at the end of my career, at university.

I could not have contemplated the teacher training without Val. She supported me financially, in practical ways and, most importantly, she encouraged me to 'stick at it' on those occasions when I began to doubt my ability to make it! She was as delighted as I was when in 1969 I finally completed the course and obtained my first post in a rural primary school, close enough to Exeter to enable daily commuting by car.

The following years were very happy ones for both of us. I had bought a very old Volkswagen Beetle car on the grounds that it was economical, quite reliable and easy for me to service myself! It took me to work each day after I had dropped Val off in the city centre, and we were a very, very happily married couple. We enjoyed life to the full in so many ways.

While continuing to work full time herself, Val maintained our little cottage home and began to play an increasing role in my teaching career. She would attend all fetes, sports days and open days, to support me. She got on well with my head teacher and my teacher colleagues and she was always there for me with help and good advice. In the early seventies, she was there standing beside me when I took my primary school class to see Prince Charles, who was on a visit as the Baron of Bradninch (one of his many titles linked to the Duchy of Cornwall) to my school. I recently came across a photo of this occasion, and it certainly brings back fond memories of my early teaching years.

Although teachers' salaries in those days did not make us rich, we managed to enjoy a reasonable social life. We went out with friends and could enjoy the odd meal out and cinema visit. Val's love of music meant a visit from time to time to the Great Hall of the university for a concert, where we once saw the great Russian pianist Vladimir Ashkenazy. We also worked my old car hard at weekends with trips to the local seaside and even to Dartmoor and Cornwall. Happy times indeed!

In 1973, I moved schools, obtaining a minor post of responsibility at a middle school in Exeter. This meant no more commuting and a small rise in my salary, so things were looking up for us! We continued to have a good life together. This new post for me was the catalyst for our first house move as a married couple.

In the early years of my teaching career, my new profession dominated both of our lives. I was full of enthusiasm and ideas! Determined to make a success of things, my life was dominated by my new job and new responsibilities to a class of forty primary school children. To be fair, Val was very supportive. Although working full time, she would always put me first. She wanted to know all about the children, what had happened in the day, what had happened in my classroom each day and how my lessons had gone.

She was not only interested but she also gave me a lot of practical support in preparing equipment to use in my lessons. It helped that she worked for WHSmith at the time! When I talked of needing lots of sticky coloured paper, counters or coloured crayons for a maths lesson, as if by magic, things would appear the following day! She bought things for me and I was so grateful that my primary school's limited budget was saved pounds by her thoughtfulness and generosity. She did get a staff discount but it was all her money and she loved doing it.

Just prior to my leaving the RAF in 1967, Val's mother had been ill and she was diagnosed with motor neurone disease. This dreadful illness is terminal and results in the patient's slow decline, usually over a period of months or at the most, a year or so. As I have indicated elsewhere, Val was much closer to her mother than to her father. It was her father who was the cause of the trouble and the physical abuse and violence in his marriage. Val as a little girl and later as a teenager not only received physical abuse herself, but as she grew older, she had to try to keep her parents' marriage together, to keep the peace. After we were married, this was a difficult role for her

With the arrival of her mother's terminal illness, Val was faced with more sadness and anguish. I did my best to support her in any way that I could. We discussed the options and came up with a compromise that would allow Val to do all that she could to care for her mother and still keep our own home and marriage strong. As a result, she moved to part-time work at Smiths and we made some changes in our daily life. Luckily, we were still in our little cottage, which was only a short walk from her mother's house. I had taken the temporary job as a civil servant and for several months we managed to cope. I was able to help in small ways.

We no longer managed to have many lunchtimes together, as Val was at her mum's bedside. We would meet sometimes at our own home and Val would spend an hour with me before returning to sit with her dying mother. I did have Fluffy, our cat, for company, and I would go with Val to visit her mother on occasion. As the year moved on, it was very sad to see the effect it had on my darling wife. I managed to tolerate being in her father's presence with difficulty at times. One thing that I do know is that Val was, in the circumstances, a wonderfully caring daughter; she nursed her mum, kept our home going and continued to work part time as a bookseller.

The last few weeks of her mother's life were terribly difficult. It was understandable that Val wanted to be with her as much as possible. She had to tolerate her father's presence there and she even prepared meals for him. Her mother had difficulty speaking by this time, but she did try to communicate to Val via words and scribbled written messages. Near her end, she told Val that she was so glad that her daughter was happily married to me and that she was pleased that I was training to be a teacher. This made my Valerie very happy, and I was also delighted when she tearfully told me. Evidently, her mother had also told her that she regretted not leaving her father, and regretted the opposition to our marriage and her part in Val's unhappy childhood. We were both warmed and comforted by these statements.

That her mother, dying in the most frightening way, could make such a confession to her daughter, literally on her deathbed, was quite remarkable. I did my best to comfort Val through these days and I made sure that she spent all the time she wanted with her mother and didn't have to worry about looking after me.

After her mother's funeral early in 1968, I wondered how Val would react and feel about her now widowed father. He quickly adapted to his new freedom. Sad to say, he began to relish the opportunities presented to him. He began to lead a rather secretive social life, which involved other women, and he was not too interested in his only daughter's feelings. Val knew how I felt about her father and that I could not forgive him for his physical abuse towards her as a child.

The problem for me was that I hoped Val would use the death of her mother as a reason to gradually distance herself from him. I underestimated my darling wife, however. She told me in no uncertain terms that she would do her best to care for her father, although she could never forgive him herself. He was her father and it was her Christian duty to care for him. She told me that she hoped I would understand and not let it become a 'thorn' between us in our marriage. I reluctantly agreed and for more than twenty-six years, I managed to keep my promise to her.

Although there were some incidents and occasions when I came close to real physical violence towards her father, I accepted that this was what Val wanted, and my task in life was to make her happy. Sometimes, over those many years, it was very difficult for me to 'turn the other cheek' and walk away. My dear wife knew this and she constantly thanked me for it. She told me that she was certain that many husbands would not be able to follow such a path and would have caused trouble or even walked out of the door!

There were times when we both really discovered how strong our love and our marriage were. Looking back now, I am so glad that I was able to maintain such behaviour. Our love for each other enabled me to comfort her when her father upset her over the years. Thankfully, Val did listen to my advice regarding caring for her father. She gradually modified some things. Although she worried about him and cared for him until his death on 2nd January 1994 in an Exeter care home, our own marriage remained intact and stronger than ever throughout these years. I insisted on our marriage being paramount; so we continued to travel regularly and do what we thought was right for us, while allowing Val to fulfil what she saw as her Christian duty. When I now think back to how Val looked after the father who had physically abused her, for more than twenty-six years, I am amazed. What a wonderful example to us all of Christianity and of faith in action. Of course, I knew that Valerie was a special kind of person, the love of my life!

On the occasions that we visited the Holy Land, five times during the period 1984 to 1994, I know that Val recharged her 'Christian batteries' there. She would return home with renewed faith and I know that she still included her father in her daily prayers. The really strange thing about Val's adult relationship with her father is the fact that few people were aware of what he had been responsible for. Valerie would never open up and talk about her childhood to anyone, except me. Another fact was she dared me to talk about it too. I was sworn to silence on such matters. Close members of her family and many friends did not know that anything untoward had happened in her life previously. She kept it all to herself until the day she died. I vowed to myself that when the time was right, I would make sure it was all revealed. Too many cases of child neglect, physical abuse and violence in marriage are swept under the carpet and ignored. It is wrong in my view; too many people suffer in silence and pay the penalty throughout their lives.

Many people, friends and family of Val and I, have been rather shocked by these revelations. In a way, it is a wonderful testament to Valerie that she was able to keep such things to herself, as is the remarkable way that she forgave her father by her actions and deeds throughout her life. Some readers may quite possibly now be wondering how they didn't know that Val's friendly, amusing bonhomie father could have been responsible for all the lies, cruelty and physical violence to his wife and only daughter, and infidelity in his marriage, to name but a few things. I have personally struggled with this dilemma. Should one 'not speak ill of the dead'? My return to a strong faith has helped. I believe the Almighty has given me sound guidance, as always, and that it is His wish that I am still here to write this.

I must return to the biographic memoir of Val and I; a love story. By the end of 1968, another sad occasion had happened. My maternal grandfather, Joseph Edmonds, had died, in June of 1968 at the age of ninety-four. I loved him dearly and so did Val. She had grown fond of him from our courting days and we were both so proud to see him and my grandmother at our wedding in 1957. He was a Great War and Boer War soldier and a highly decorated war hero. Many years later, I noticed a photo of my grandfather in the Exeter paper *The Express & Echo*, and this resulted in a subsequent article that I wrote about his military career, which was published in the same paper. It was a little bit of fame at last for a modest, wonderful man who had done so much not only for me, but so many in his long life. Val was very upset attending two funerals in a few months, of people who meant so much to her.

We had settled back into our life by the year 1970. Val was still caring for her father on a daily basis, punctuated by our weekends away in Cornwall and at least two or three holidays each year. Luckily, her father liked his freedom and there were even times when he travelled back to his original roots in Yorkshire, where he had family still living. I was now working at a middle school in Exeter, and in the early 1970s, we began to think of moving to a larger and newer house! We had noticed that a lot of new houses were being built in the Exwick area of Exeter, and we began the exciting task of looking at new houses within our price range, across the city.

Val really loved it! For the first time in our lives, we could hope to buy a new property and for many weeks we pursued that dream. Looking at all the newspapers, visiting agents and driving around sites became our norm for the weekends and many evenings. I remember that we even thought of moving out to the countryside, and we soon became much more familiar with some of Exeter's commuter villages. We put our little cottage on the market and things began to move quickly.

In 1973, our dream of a new house came true. We sold our small and much-loved cottage in Bonhay Road and moved to a three-bedroom semi on a new development in Exwick: 68 Rowan Way. Although brand new, the house had its problems. There were unfinished bits in the house, top soil had not been delivered for the rear garden, and the sloping drive to the garage was very frightening. As seemed to be the norm at the time, after our solicitors had chased the builders, they went out of business! We were left with a paper so-called ten-year guarantee, which was, in reality, useless. Nevertheless, Val and I were delighted, very happy, and with our now very elderly cat, Fluffy, in residence, we started settling in. Tall fences for the rear garden were a priority so that Fluffy would feel safe. Soil was obtained and I even did manage to get my car in the garage! Val was so excited at that time. She loved getting curtains and furnishing our new and much larger home.

Fate decided that we were only to live at 68 Rowan Way for seven years. They were important years in our marriage, however, and another step in my sworn vow to give my darling wife all that she wanted, whenever possible. It was another of her dreams that had come true, a brand-new home in a very pleasant location overlooking the City of Exeter.

The seven years that we lived in our new home in Rowan Way were made much happier because we had very good neighbours. Two of these, the Moggeridges and the Wilsons, became close friends and remained so for more than forty years. These friendships continued throughout our sixteen years living in St David's and our twenty-three years in Dawlish until Val's death in 2019.

Marion and Stewart Moggeridge lived next door to us and were very friendly and welcoming. They had a small son at the time, Mark, when we moved, but the addition of a daughter, Melanie, when we left! An indication of the length and closeness of our friendship with these lovely people is that Val and I attended the weddings of both Mark and Melanie, in different parts of the country, many years later. Melanie's wedding was particularly poignant for Val because she had been present at her home birth in Rowan Way.

The Wilsons lived one house down from us and were also to become good friends. They moved in at number 72 about six months after us, and their arrival caused something of a stir in the road! This was because Bob Wilson happened to be the newly signed professional goalkeeper for Exeter City FC. Bob was well over six feet tall and Maureen, his wife, a blonde bombshell! You could almost 'hear' the excitement among our neighbours in the early days after their arrival.

Val and I were quite unaware of the Wilsons' arrival in the first few days, although I had been a local football supporter for many years. We discovered our new neighbours in a rather bizarre manner. My father had taken to making random visits to us in his old Ford car on a Sunday morning. The weekend after the Wilsons had moved in, our quiet cups of coffee were to be interrupted when my father arrived, breathless with excitement.

"You didn't tell me City's goalkeeper was your new neighbour!"

He had spotted Bob working on his Triumph 2000 Saloon on his driveway, recognised him immediately and was obviously thrilled. We explained that it was all news to us, and the conversation was dominated thereafter by football and our new neighbours.

Trying to be polite and retain some dignity, Val and I didn't rush down to the Wilsons' house and introduce ourselves. We waited for an opportune moment when we just happened to be in our front garden when Bob appeared! A wave of welcome was enough. Being the football fan, I took the lead in the introductions as Val soon came on the scene, soon to be followed by Maureen Wilson's appearance, cradling Pepe, their white poodle dog, in her arms. We all made a fuss of the dog, of course, in our small talk, but it was not long before I confessed to being an avid supporter of Bob's new team. That gave us common ground for a lengthy conversation while our two wives went indoors to share domestic problems common in moving into newly built houses.

Over the following few weeks, we met several times in alternate houses, in the evenings, for a quiet drink and many long chats. I discovered that Bob and Maureen had already been in Exeter for some months, living in an Exeter City FC house, while he was on loan from his parent club, Cardiff City. He had recently signed a three-year contract, so the couple had decided to buy a new house in Rowan Way, just like Val and I. We seemed to get on well, instantly having similar values and a sense of humour. Add to that my interest in football and my father being a season-ticket holder at St James' Park, plus Val's natural caring nature, and it's no wonder we got on. We all liked animals too so that helped. During our chats, we discovered that we were of similar ages, although we were slightly older by a few years; that Bob and Maureen were both from Birmingham; that Bob's first professional team was Aston Villa and that he had travelled the world with Cardiff City in European Cup games, while he was the first-team goalkeeper for them. Naturally, I was intrigued to listen to all football history. Our get-togethers helped to make our settling-in at Rowan Way more comfortable and easier for all four of us.

Over the seven years living in Rowan Way, we socialised with Bob and Maureen Wilson regularly. This included meals out together, meals in each other's houses and one or two rather memorable 'football parties'!

The first took place in Plymouth; Exeter City, Torquay United and Plymouth Argyle were competing in a five-a-side football tournament hosted by Argyle. Val and I travelled down to the sports arena venue with Bob and Maureen in their car, in the afternoon, at their invitation. We attended the event in the evening and it was good to enjoy VIP status with reserved seats, and so on. Bob was Exeter's goalkeeper on the night, so after the tournament finished, Maureen, Val and I had quite a long wait for Bob to get changed, showered and back with us. That was when we began to sense 'footballers' party spirit'. Players, wives and girlfriends, plus guests like Val and I, team officials, managers, directors and so on, all headed for the Barbican area of Plymouth. I wouldn't be able to find my way there now, I am sure. At the time, Val and I thought we were in the USA as we remembered going through various doors, where we were checked by security staff who resembled something out of the sleazy parts of New York or Las Vegas. We eventually entered a large room with bar, live music band, lots of noise and dancing! We had never seen anything like it before. Most of the footballers I recognised were dancing with young women, some wives, I was told. Many had obviously been drinking for some time and were certainly letting their hair down, to say the least. As we moved into the room and Bob set off to get us drinks, I noticed that Val was staying very close to me and gripping my hand tightly. Maureen Wilson had seen it all before and was behaving as if it was an everyday experience for her; it most certainly wasn't for Val and me! We did enjoy the whole day-and-night event. It was an education for us about footballers' 'out-of-hours' behaviour, so to speak! This was, remember, in the 1970s. I suspect it is all rather different today!

The second party I remember clearly was a different event. It was held at a player's house and garden but it was very enjoyable, especially as it enabled Val and me to meet and talk to so many players informally. There were some from Exeter, Torquay and Plymouth, of course, but also some from larger clubs in the league, and some managers. There were several International players there, whom I had only seen on the TV screen! Over the years, I made the acquaintance of many players through our friendship with the Wilsons.

After a few years in Rowan Way, we continued our friendship with the Wilsons. Maureen Wilson was working part time like Val and they would often have a cup of tea together at home, after work. Val was still preparing meals for her father and made daily trips on foot to St David's. During this time, Bob Wilson asked me if I would mind giving a lift to his wife to the football ground on a Saturday when there was a home game. He knew I drove there myself regularly. Val never raved about football at any time. Maureen had complained to Bob about sitting alone in a draughty grandstand at St James' Park for an hour or more before a game; her husband, as a player, had to be there early. I readily agreed and I also then had a free ticket in the stand from Bob each week as a gift. Val didn't mind. The only trouble was that I ended up sitting beside several players' wives and partners each week, at home games, learning a lot of new things about footballers' wives in the process. These wives did not like to see their husbands kicked, injured or even 'booed' on occasion!

I remember a notable anecdote from this time. Val came home from work one day and greeted me with this tale. A work colleague told Val that she had some bad news for her. She took Val to one side and seemed embarrassed at the time.

"I'm sorry to have to tell you, Val, but your John is having an affair."

A flabbergasted Val demanded an explanation.

"I've seen him with an attractive blonde in his car, in the front seat."

Suddenly Val realised what this was all about.

"Was it a Saturday when you saw them?" asked Val.

"Yes, three separate Saturdays, always the same woman."

Val explained to the woman that I was giving a lift to a neighbour's wife, a footballer. Luckily, Val took it well, as I knew she would, but I was more upset at the thought of how easily rumours can be created and things taken out of context.

Sadly, the blonde lady referred to above, Maureen Wilson, died of cancer in her early forties. Val and I visited her in Frenchay Hospital, Bristol, before she died, and we both attended her funeral. Luckily, Bob found new love and married again, a lovely lady called Dee, and Val and I continued to be friends with them for many years.

A postscript to this piece of writing is that sadly Bob Wilson himself passed away recently after a heart attack. As we are still in the middle of the COVID pandemic, restrictions on funerals and assemblies still apply, so I have not been able to pay my respects properly to someone who was kind, caring and a dear friend to Val and me for over more than forty years.

After Val's death in 2019, Bob and Dee Wilson attended both her funeral and the Celebration of her Life event. They continued their friendship and kindness to me personally in the following months. Bob even came down to Dawlish to collect me and take me to an Exeter City FC game at St James' Park, where I enjoyed a stand seat and also met again footballers like Alan Banks, Jimmy Giles, Jimmy Blain and Johnny Hore. He then drove me back to Dawlish after the game. He was a gentleman, a good professional footballer with a wicked sense of humour and a dear friend who will not be forgotten.

Those years living in our new house in Exwick were certainly eventful and happy years. I was teaching in Exeter, so travel was not a problem for me. Val was performing miracles, as usual. She was working full time at Smiths, she was looking after me and our home in Rowan Way and also looking after her now widowed father in St David's. How she did it all with a smile on her face, I will never know. She was happy in her work, where she was popular, and she had many good friends. She was also happy turning our new house into a home, where we thankfully had good neighbours. As I saw it, the only dark side to our life at that time was Val's father, an ever-present reminder to Val and me of things best forgotten and moved away from, but because of Val's Christian beliefs, this was impossible to do. Val was adamant that she had a duty to look after him and do the best she could for him. She visited him daily and tidied his house in Tavistock Road, and she provided him with a cooked meal every day. She did this while working full time, keeping our house maintained and looking after me! What is more, she used to walk to work from Rowan Way, Exwick via the railway crossing to her father's house in Tavistock Road, St David's. From there, she would walk up to her work at WHSmith. My car journey to my school was a comparative doddle. although I would often drop Val off in the St David's area to help her when she was taking her prepared meals to her father.

There was no danger of Val putting on any weight! She was a little dynamo and miraculously she kept healthy throughout these years. I must confess that I was not happy with the situation, particularly when her father decided on occasion to visit us at weekends, just when Sunday lunch was being served! I was aware that if I was not careful, the 'Father-in-Law' element creeping into and affecting our marriage would do some damage to us as a couple. Constantly thinking about what he had been responsible for in Val's childhood, I found it difficult to be even civil to her father on occasion. Val always managed to defuse the tension and often her father would take the hint from me and leave suddenly. Val and I inevitably had some long and sometimes quite emotional conversations about the situation we found ourselves in at this time.

Val was so grateful and she thanked me constantly for putting up with it all regarding her father. She knew how difficult it was for me, and because of our love, we weathered the storm of those years somehow. We did both realise that it could not go on like this for too long. Val accepted that she could not continue to do all she was doing on a daily basis. Reluctantly, she negotiated with WHSmith to work on a part-time contract and I was delighted for her and for us. It enabled Val to use some of her afternoons or days off to tend to her father in his own house. She knew that this would mean less contact and friction for me. It still meant a lot of extra work for Val every day, of course, and frequent walks from Exwick to St David's. It did, however, ease the growing tension between us over her father, which I was deeply worried about at the time. I did not have to be in his physical presence so much and we started to find that our marriage benefitted considerably. I remained very concerned about Val and all that she was trying to do, afraid that it would adversely affect her both physically and emotionally.

Although the shadow of her father remained with us, thankfully, it did not damage our marriage; we still enjoyed life together and in spite of everything our marriage was strong and indeed thrived. As frequently happens, adversity and problems brought us closer together. We found time to spend together sitting on a sofa with our arms around one another, in an evening, with a glass of wine. Often, we would find ourselves remembering past holidays and events with considerable pleasure and sometimes humour. Importantly, we would share little anecdotes from the day's events. For Val, it would usually be from her work. She was always careful not to recount her daily time with her father to me. For me, it was always my school day and lessons. So that I could make Val's day easier, I did not drive home for lunch, making do with some sandwiches or even a school dinner on occasion! Sometimes, we would spend the evenings watching TV together or planning our next getaway holiday or weekend. Our long-time hobbies, which we had both pursued in our small cottage, were sadly neglected at the time.

Val still enjoyed her reading, which she had to keep going as part of her work as a bookseller, and she continued with her ever-present love of music. All our homes together always had plenty of books and music in them. As any teacher will know, there were also many evenings when I spent hours just marking piles of exercise books and preparing lessons. Val was a darling in always giving me the necessary time and space for my schoolwork and never complaining about it.

My profession and schools did sometimes provide us, however, as a couple, with some light relief and entertainment. It wasn't all work! There was occasionally some play! We attended some really good parties during these years, particularly during my time at Hele's School in Exeter. I had the unique distinction of returning to the school that I attended as a pupil, as a member of the teaching staff! This needs some clarification. The school that I attended as a teenager was Hele's Boys' Grammar School, located at the time in St David's, Exeter. The school at which I took up a teaching post was Hele's Boys' Comprehensive School at Southam in Exeter. Quite a different place, of course; nevertheless, it was fundamentally the same school reorganised during the education revolution in the '50s and '60s. I joined two other Old Heleans on the staff at the comp. school. It was fascinating to discover, on my first day, that three of my teachers from the 1940/50 period were still there in post! I hasten to add that I did not address them as 'Sir' anymore, but we did enjoy some happy chats together.

Val and I enjoyed several Hele's staff parties, including some at Exeter Golf Club with the use of the swimming pool; also a couple of very memorable fancy dress parties. On one notable occasion at the golf club, I remember us having to beat a hasty retreat when things got too much, particularly for Val! This was when, late at night, after a meal and a lot of wine, some younger staff members and a few wives decided to go for a swim without the benefit of swimming costumes. Needless to say, we didn't attend many staff parties after that.

On the subject of school staff parties, another notable occasion comes to mind. I was teaching at another school in Exeter, which shall remain nameless, when Val and I were invited to a private party at the home of a member of staff. This was a large luxurious bungalow set in its own grounds in the depths of the country a few miles from Exeter. The male staff member who issued the invitation to me was married to the head teacher of another school in a different area of Devon. I made discreet enquiries about the nature of these parties, keen to know more before accepting the invite. Female members of staff were lavish in their praise, describing the food as excellent, music professional and usually a great time was had by all. I discussed the invite with Val at some length and we decided not to go.

A little later in the year, I was approached once again by the same staff colleague who enthused about his parties and pleaded with me to go to the next one, with my wife, of course. By this time, Val and I had been to one or two school-based events, prize days and a dinner. When I arrived home with the new party invitation, Val surprised me by insisting I sit down with her and discuss it. She then informed me that at the various school-based events she had attended with me, she had talked to some of the female teachers and some wives about the 'famous' parties. She told me that she had got the distinct impression from her conversations at the school that these parties were rather risqué events in that they often turned into all-night sessions, with wife-swapping not unknown! I was quite shocked on hearing this.

We did eventually, some months later, pluck up the courage to accept one of the ongoing invitations; however, we took the precaution of pre-booking a taxi for ourselves at a reasonable hour so that there was no danger of us staying late or all night! In fact, I believe that the rumours Val had heard about the parties were quite unfounded. We enjoyed it overall. The food was excellent and the music good. We ignored the invitation to join some couples for an evening swim in the private pool, not having brought swimming gear with us. I made sure throughout the evening that I monopolised Val as my partner on the dance floor, with only one or two exceptions. That was, if I am honest, one of the few occasions in my life when I was ever propositioned by another man's wife. An attractive young lady, she managed to get Val's okay to dance with me. It was a smoochy dance to a slow Neil Diamond number. Her body language said it all, together with her whispered words in my ear, which were more explicit. I was downright embarrassed at the way she was throwing herself at me, and I was extremely grateful for the dark lighting and shadows to hide in as we made our slow way around the large area. I hoped that the dim lighting would shield it all from Val. Not so, of course. When I had disentangled myself from this woman and returned to Val, I was immediately aware that my darling wife was not amused!

"She was coming on to you. Do you fancy her or something?" The words were quite chilling from Val.

My reaction was to grab Val in a close embrace and quickly join the next dance. Val proceeded to then give me a great loving 'over-the-top' performance of clinging to me for the rest of our time there. We did actually laugh a lot in the taxi on our way home, and we decided to cut down on our party-going in the future, particularly any teachers' parties in remote locations in the country!

In 1978, Val and I had an overnight stay in Plymouth as a treat for ourselves. We managed to get tickets to see the 1950s popular US singer Frankie Laine. We had both grown up during the 'pop' musical age of Laine, Sinatra, Como, Nat King Cole and Johnny Mathis. All through our courting years, we constantly played their records, so it was a nostalgic trip for us. We enjoyed the nightclub concert where we watched Frankie Laine perform some of his many chart-topping songs of the fifties and early sixties. We were taken back in time listening to *Jezebel, I Believe, Jealousy* and the many songs that he recorded for films and TV, like *Blowing Wild, Gunfight at the O.K. Corral* and *Rawhide*.

What really made the night special for us was the fact that we were able to meet the singer backstage after the show. He was taken with Val when she told him that she had sold thousands of his records in the 1950s, as the manager of a record department. She could even tell him the UK numbers of his greatest hits on the Columbia and Philips labels!

He autographed an LP record for us there and then – '*To Val and John with thanks*'. We then had a photo taken with him. A memorable night, indeed.

We continued to have a happy life in our newly built house in Rowan Way. There was, however, a constant shadow in the background. Val's father still had a significant influence on both of us. I was personally always unhappy when he was around; I could not forget what he had been responsible for during Val's childhood. It was always difficult to keep my emotions and even anger under control and concealed. This made for some uncomfortable days when he was with us. Val's insistence that she had a Christian duty to continue to care for him was paramount. She always tried hard to think of me and she understood my feelings about it all, but she was adamant that she would continue to do it.

Although she did her best to avoid me being in his presence, it still happened and it was upsetting for both of us.

Most days, she would take a cooked meal to him in his own house, but he would still appear in his car outside our house at weekends. This would inevitably result in Val inviting him to have lunch with us with the attendant stress that entailed. An added strain for me was the indifference with which he treated Val. I was very angry when I discovered that he often didn't even bother to eat the cooked meals that Val had prepared for him during the week. She would find them in his dustbin when she was cleaning his house.

Val's daily routine consisted of working as a bookseller part time at WHSmith, preparing a cooked meal for her father, delivering it to his home, collecting his laundry, then returning to our home and repeating this all over again for us, with more cooking and cleaning.

Meanwhile, I was away all day pursuing my teaching career. This state of affairs continued for many years and we were both aware that it could not go on forever. It is true that we did manage to have some breaks. We needed them! We made a point of taking some weekends off and travelling down to St Buryan in Cornwall; and when we were blessed with school holiday time, we went further afield. I can remember Val making telephone calls to her father even when we were in Cornwall or Scotland, just to see that he was okay. Even then, he often didn't answer her calls every time, causing her to worry unnecessarily about his welfare. That annoyed me considerably.

In a way, fate intervened in our marriage once again to alleviate some of this stress and unhappiness. We discovered by accident that a house had come on the market in the St David's area of Exeter and it was located quite close to Val's father's house, her old home. It was the largest house in the area and the former premises of a long-established family-owned taxi business. As such, it had a brick-built self-contained office at the rear, together with ample parking off road, double door access to the rear and a decent-sized garden. The taxi firm had been operating in this location for many years, and as Val had been living nearby for most of her life, she knew it well. When we heard about its availability, it gave us something to think about.

Over several weeks, we discussed the pros and cons of making an offer on this property. It was a difficult time for us in many ways. After all, it had been our dream to move into a newly built house as the first owners. We had now achieved that and we liked the area and our neighbours. We really did not want to leave 68 Rowan Way. However, we knew that while her father was alive, Val would continue to look after him and I had to accept that. I also knew that she was under a great strain, physically and mentally, and that it would take its toll on her, and us. A move to a house nearer her father's offered some sort of solution. It would help ease Val's daily load of work and travel, and hopefully some of the stress she was under. It did offer us a larger, although older, house with some extras. The taxi office at the rear could be my study for schoolwork and also perhaps enable me to restart my long-time hobby of amateur radio. There was ample parking, two toilets and spacious high-ceilinged rooms. The whole house was well decorated, with expensive carpets, and the kitchen was more than four times larger than our modern one in Rowan Way.

Eventually, we decided to go for it and make an offer on the St David's property. We put our house on the market and started proceedings to move. We were sad leaving Rowan Way after only seven years there but, in the circumstances, I think we made the right decision at the time. Val would be able to reach her old home where her now widowed father still lived in a matter of minutes; she had an easier walk to her morning's work and access to local shops and a post office. She also had a spacious house with a large kitchen and spare bedrooms, and I had a detached brick-built office or study of my own! An added bonus for both of us was the fact that our new house was five minutes' walk away from St David's train station and a mainline rail service. We were to make good use of that facility over the sixteen years we spent living in St David's! Another good thing for Val was that she still had some of her family living close by for some sort of support. In particular, her late mother's sister, Vera, Val's favourite aunt, lived nearby.

We made the move to the house in St David's late in 1980. Luckily, there was very little decorating to do there and we settled in quite well. Val's father thought that it was great for him to have her close by at his beck and call. I had to take swift action and make it clear to him that this was not going to happen and that he was not going to be welcome in our house on a daily basis. Although I was not too explicit, I also let him know in no uncertain terms that my attitude towards him had not changed. Val would continue to visit him daily and provide meals for him, do his washing and keep his house clean. That was her choice. No way was I going to tolerate him using our home as and when he wanted to. Fortunately, he got the message loud and clear from me. I am pleased to say that Val accepted my 'rules' regarding her father visiting us. I knew that it would cause trouble if I saw too much of him. She made sure that any invites she made to him were very limited and during the daytime when I was not there. I knew that he would manage to call on her during the day when I was not there, but I could safely turn a blind eye to that. I still marvel to this day at the way Val could still be so kind to him, for so long. She was a wonderful example of practical Christian forgiveness and caring.

One thing that did help to ease all the stress for both of us was that Val managed to develop some new skills and interests. Our house in St David's was large and well appointed when we moved in. Val added to its décor with her own artistic flair. She improved the house over the first few years with additional furniture, chandeliers and paintings, all of which considerably enhanced the look of the place. The large lounge, which contained Val's piano, offered quite luxurious and comfortable surroundings for any guests. We bought large and very well-framed paintings for the main rooms, which added some class, thanks to Val. I recall a large Bernard Buffet and a Turner dominated the walls; Val's informed choice, of course!

Alongside this achievement of making the house into our 'home', she also expanded her culinary skills in her very large kitchen. Inevitably, this led to us entertaining more at home. Val became very good at being the hostess and she developed many new skills too. In the kitchen, she recalled all that she had learned in the Far East. Indonesian and Malay dishes became the norm for us on a weekly basis; they also became very popular with our friends and other guests. Val's curries were to become quite famous, so much so that some friends would demand she cooked them one when they came to dine with us. The fact that the basic curry and rice was accompanied by a tray of up to ten different condiments or additions, including raw pineapple and six or seven spicy chutneys, mango and banana, always made for a welcome feast! Val also bought new cutlery, wine glasses, napkins, tablecloths and even a silver candelabra for her table displays. We entertained a lot over these years.

During the early years at the St David's house, we provided accommodation for Fred and Ruby Downey, our friends from Toronto in Canada. They were on a nostalgic visit to the UK, where Fred had been stationed with the Canadian forces prior to D-Day in June 1944. In 1982, they returned our hospitality and entertained us when we were on our silver wedding trip to Canada, recorded elsewhere in this book.

Another notable occasion was when Val decided to lay on a dinner for my parents' Golden Wedding Anniversary. It was a surprise for them and they were amazed at all the fuss we went to that day for them. Val produced a great meal with all the trimmings and a professionally made cake for the occasion. It was a lovely evening and very special, as my father's only sister, my Aunt Gladys, attended. She was a frail widow at the time but she made the effort to attend, dressing up for the occasion. She added much to the evening with her memories of my father and herself as children growing up in Perth, Scotland. My mother's younger brother, my Uncle Bill, was also there. In all, it was a first-class night, thanks to Val's hard work and her caring nature. She loved to make others happy in special ways throughout her life. The glowing tribute and kind words about Val that my Aunt Gladys said to me as I drove her home after the dinner still remain clearly in my mind today.

The fact that we had two large spare bedrooms at the time also helped. We were able to provide accommodation for the children of many overseas friends when they were on holiday in the UK. This included Mary and Micky Smyth from Perth, Australia. They were two of John and Jennifer Smyth's children, who had been good friends of ours in Exeter when they lived here. John Smyth was a doctor at the RD& E Hospital for many years, and a consultant, who emigrated to Australia. We kept in touch by phone and letters over the years and they visited the UK regularly; we often met up for a meal in Exeter.

Another example of our entertaining during these years living in St David's further illustrates Val's kindness to others. She was working in Pitts bookshop in Exeter at the time. Although only a part-time employee, she got on well with all of the staff there. It came to her attention that one of the staff there, a divorcee, Jennifer, was leaving. This lady was emigrating to Australia, where she was going to join her married daughter who lived there. Val decided that she would make her departure memorable by throwing a party for her and for all the female staff, at our house. She organised it all herself and paid for everything. I'll be honest, I wasn't too keen, but I agreed in the end simply to make my Val happy. It was a Wednesday night, I recall; and as I was banned from the house for the evening – it was an all-female night – I took myself off with some mates to St James' Park to watch a midweek football match.

Val was cooking all day in her large kitchen. She prepared a lovely cooked meal, provided drinks and set up a party table for eight ladies. She even decorated our large lounge with various Australian toy kangaroos and koalas plus lots of Aussie flags everywhere.

After my football game, I had a few drinks with my mates and then walked home to St David's. Arriving home at about ten thirty, I found the party still in full swing. I had to put up with introductions to seven excited ladies, which was somewhat overwhelming! I have recently found some photos of that occasion, taken by Val. The party was a great success and Val was very happy. I was glad that night that we had a large house, plenty of room and two toilets!

Sadly, throughout these years, Val learned a lot more about her father. Suspicions that she had about his earlier life were confirmed. When she carried on looking after him as a daughter, she discovered that he was still having affairs, telling lies about her and that he didn't really have any feelings for her. She also discovered that he had been married before he met her mother; that he had abandoned his first wife in Yorkshire and that she probably had unknown siblings there. These shocking revelations that came to light over time still did not stop her doing her Christian duty towards him. Today, I still find that quite remarkable.

My one consoling thought is that although he treated his daughter so cruelly through her childhood, and later, he did not in a sense win. Val escaped in her marriage to me; we had a great life together and she knew true happiness for more than sixty-one years.

On a happier note, our adopted cat 'Lavender' moved with us to St David's, and she was a great comfort to Val. Although in a poor state of health due to the cruelty she had experienced earlier, Lavender was given a good final few years of life by Val and I. She had the best vet in town to look after her health, good food, warm rooms and frequent laps to snooze upon.

There is so much more that I could reveal about Val's father and the way that he treated her, both in her early life and later. However, I do not intend to do so. It would be contrary to my stated aims in writing this book as our love story. Although Val's father still cast a shadow over many years of our marriage, we managed to steer a course through it all successfully.

Val continued to do what she saw as her Christian duty in 1992 when her father was diagnosed with Alzheimer's disease; she arranged for him to have a place in a care home, where she visited him regularly. She also arranged and financed his funeral two years later when he died at the age of eighty-seven. I attended his funeral, not out of respect for him, but to support Val. It is significant that after his death and throughout his funeral and burial, his only daughter of his second marriage, my dear wife, Val, did not shed one tear.

She told me afterwards what she really thought of him and more of what he had done to her and her mother. She could not bring herself to say it while he still lived, but she could never forgive him. I personally know, because I witnessed it, that Val did more than most people could ever have done for a man who, she told me after his death, was a 'rotter', the strongest word she could find to express herself on the subject. Unlike most families, we rarely did mention her father again in the following twenty-five years of our marriage.

Two years after her father's death, we began to think about our future. I was teaching full time in Somerset and Val was working part time at Waterstones bookshop in Exeter. This continued for another two years until, in 1996, we started to think about finding a retirement bungalow somewhere. To remain in a large house in St David's was no longer sensible. Val was free of her obligations to her father, at last, and the choice was now ours. Actually, that was not quite true. I had already decided in my mind that Valerie could decide where we went, but I didn't tell her so! Eventually, she let me know that she would like to retire to the seaside, so that meant either Exmouth and East Devon or Dawlish and South Devon. Val chose Dawlish, which, as the reader will already know, had special memories for us, at the Dawlish Warren, Shutterton Lane end!

In the autumn of 1996, we moved to a bungalow in Lower Drive, Dawlish, where we spent a further twenty-four years together and where I still reside. We were not to know that the year after we moved to Dawlish I was to be struck down with a life-threatening cancer.

Already several times in my writing, I have mentioned the fact that I had a major underlying aim throughout our marriage of doing my best to fulfil all Val's dreams. I was constantly aware of this. I felt that I had to do all that I could to compensate for her unhappy childhood, to make her happy and to express my love for her at all times. As a result of her sad, lonely and unhappy early life, Val needed to escape that world, and extensive travel offered therapy, a cure and a significant step on her personal road to a happy life.

In fifty-eight of our sixty-one years of marriage, we did travel a lot. On reflection, I can honestly say that I could not have done more to fulfil that goal for her. One of the many things that have been a great comfort to me during the months after Val's death has been various birthday, Christmas and anniversary cards that she gave me. Her choice of cards, the words printed on them, chosen with great care, and her added written words have often lifted my spirits when I've been at a low ebb. I still have more than a dozen of these cards on permanent display in my lounge. Recently, having endured a rather restless night thinking of Val and being somewhat depressed, in the morning, I decided to cheer myself up by rereading these cards. One particular card took my eye. Val had sent it to me on our fifty-second wedding anniversary in 2009. The illustration on the front shows a loving couple in a gondola in Venice sailing along a canal. We visited Venice on two occasions ourselves.

The front caption reads, '*On Our Anniversary With Love – You're the Only One There Could Ever Be*'.

The inside caption reads, '*I Love You With All My Heart – You Mean the World to Me*'.

The most striking thing for me, however, was that on the left side of the card, she had written thirty-three names of places, towns and countries that we had visited together. These were all special places for us, holding lovely memories. When she wrote it in 2009, she was seventy-three years old. The choice of card and the writing she had added herself would suggest that she had certainly been recalling the fifty-two years of our travelling together with much joy and happiness. If I needed confirmation that I had made her happy in respect of her travel dreams, I have it here!

The reader may be interested to see the whole list as written on this card by Val. Many of these places also appear elsewhere in other chapters of this book.

Deauville Greece Bethlehem Monte Carlo
Venice Edinburgh Porthcurno Belgium
Prague RY Britannia St Buryan Amsterdam
Jerusalem QE II Spittal of Glenshee
Portugal Orient Express Balmoral
Cannes London Perth
Singapore Paris Toronto
Austria Rome Niagara Falls
Penang Malta Bayeux
Berlin Bethlehem Arromanches

Today, I have a wonderful feeling of love for my Valerie-Hazel. (She signed the card like this!)

In the following two chapters, I will be recalling some of our travels. Inevitably, one cannot cover it all. However, the reader will get a glimpse of some things that we got up to during many years of happy marriage.

Chapter 7

On Our Travels – In the UK

When I was in the RAF, our holidays together had been governed by my leave dates and even, on occasion, by the destinations. There were some countries that I was not allowed to visit. Now that I was a civilian, this was no longer the case. We could plan our holidays ourselves. As my career in teaching developed, the only constraint now was the fact that we could only plan our holidays when the schools were closed. Holidays had to be planned carefully to coincide with official school holidays. As some members of my family liked to remind us, schoolteachers had lots of holidays! Compared to most professions, this is true; the fact that many of my holidays were devoted to lesson preparation and other school tasks did not enter into it! Nevertheless, Easter, Christmas and the long summer break offered many weeks for vacations. Add to that the half-term breaks and all the weekends, and it certainly gave Val and me plenty of scope for more travelling.

Much of my free time was spent in schoolwork. The weekends and many of the school breaks were not available for holidays. We both accepted this. Although the desire to travel was still very much with us, we decided to wait on this and put it off until my teaching career was fully established. In spite of this, we did manage some short holidays. Having transport, although rather ancient, allowed us some opportunities for short journeys. Some weekends we went to the seaside, enjoying sunbathing and swimming in the lovely waters close by. We were so fortunate to live in Devon and we knew it!

During these years, we also discovered the delights of simple holidays. We bought a tent and all the camping gear. Having practised putting up the tent and learning how to operate a simple gas-heater stove, we decided to try the real thing. The VW Beetle was duly packed full of all the camping gear, including newly purchased sleeping bags. Val was very keen and she insisted on filling several cardboard boxes with food and a picnic basket, complete with plastic tea set and cutlery. This had to be squeezed into an already overloaded car. I didn't say anything to Val but I secretly worried about the ability of the VW's well-worn engine to get us to Cornwall, our planned destination.

We did make it on that first camping trip. Luckily, I made sure that we stopped regularly en route down the A30, allowing the air-cooled engine to have frequent and very necessary breaks from its hard work. I kept making excuses for the stops. Telling Val that we should enjoy the view on Bodmin Moor or insisting that I had a break from driving. There were times when I also thought that I should save up for a new and better car! Val was her usual wonderful self; she smiled and loved every minute of it, seeing it as a great adventure. As usual, she was right. When we eventually drove through Penzance and on towards Land's End, we came to a small village called St Buryan. This village was to play a big part in the following forty years or so of our marriage. It became very important to both of us, together with the friends we made there on that first camping holiday.

Apart from the Holy Land, Israel, there were four more areas which tended to dominate our holiday choices over more than forty years. These were mutual favourites and we spent many memorable weeks on holiday and we never grew tired of them. Every year between the late seventies and 2016 we visited them regularly. They were the home areas in the UK of Cornwall and Scotland, plus the European areas of Austria and the South of France. We were rarely disappointed with these destinations, and we eventually felt quite at home in all of them.

Our love affair with Cornwall began early in our marriage when we made that first memorable trip in a VW Beetle down the A30. We had a tent and thanks to Val and her enthusiasm and excitement, we also had all the other camping requisites. We had never been on a camping holiday before so it was an adventure for us. It was so new to us that when we eventually arrived in West Cornwall, we hadn't even booked a campsite. It helped, no doubt, that we were young and very much in

On board the SS BENLOYAL – Singapore.

At the entrance to our flat in Singapore.

New Years Eve at the Raffles Hotel – Singapore.

Early travels – Austria.

Val at Mozart's birthplace – Austria.

With the Bradburys – silver wedding trip 1982.

At Niagara Falls on 26/10/82 Silver wedding.

'Ginger' the Bradbury's rescued cat.

Val with the Bradbury's – silver wedding trip 1982.

Val after a swim. Tel Aviv, Israel. 1994.   Enjoying a look at the Negev Desert in Israel.

Having a snack in Tel Aviv, Israel. 1984.

Wedding Day 26th October 1957.

60 Years Later. Our Diamond Wedding Day 26/10/17 at Val's Care Home.

We met American singer Frankie Laine in Plymouth. Val had sold lots of his records early in her life!

Val happy in our first caravan – she loved them!

Wrapped up well against the cold in a chilly Venice – still travelling aged 75!

love. It was not long after our life as a married couple in the services, the RAF. The freedom to go where we liked, often when we liked, was a major influence in our choice of Cornwall to embark on new holiday adventures together. It was close by and it did not cost a lot of money to get there. Our first holiday in Cornwall was quite an adventure in itself. We didn't know where we would end up. Luckily, we found the small village of St Buryan, between Penzance and Land's End. We also found Tower Farm Camping and Caravan Site for the first time. Tower Farm and the camping site were owned and run by a local Cornish farmer and his wife, Jim and Joyce Hosking. Their home, Tower Farm, was close by the camping site and they ran the site almost single-handed, assisted by some local help only.

I have fond memories of that first holiday, sleeping in a tent, cooking on a tiny gas stove and cuddling up to Val in an effort to keep warm and dry through the heavy dew-laden Cornish nights. The Hoskings were lovely people. They were warm and welcoming and it was a delight to listen to their tales of their farm life, local folklore and much of the history of the area. Val and I soon began a friendship with this couple that was to include some regular correspondence and many, many holidays at their site. An added attraction for Val was the farm's donkey called Wilbur. She loved donkeys and Wilbur was spoiled with carrots and treats regularly. During the summer season when there were lots of children there, Jim would hitch up a small trap and Wilbur would give them rides around the large campsite. These were lovely simple holidays that remain clear in my memory even today.

After a year or two of camping in a tent at Tower Park, we graduated to a serviceable but old caravan that we bought at Pathfinder Caravans and took down to West Cornwall. Val loved caravans as well as donkeys. For many years, we then had the luxury of being able to go down to St Buryan and stay in our own caravan. Jim only charged a nominal rent for leaving our caravan on his site next to his row of static vans which he rented out in the summer. In return for his kindness, we even looked after his farmhouse for a week at one time; selling eggs, keeping the place tidy and fielding many phone calls. Luckily, his son took care of the cows and milking them, I'm pleased to say! Our friendship with the Hoskings continued after they sold both the farm and the camping business. In fact, we visited them at their retirement bungalow in Penzance as late as 2015. As well as being an active dairy farmer, Jim Hosking was an eminent Cornish bard and historian, who published several books on Cornish history after he retired. There was a brief period when the Tower Park camping site changed hands several times and as a result we did not visit so often. We eventually had to remove our old caravan from the site but we still returned many times, renting a static van on the site.

We loved the area so much and it became our haven of tranquillity, peace and solitude. It was an ideal getaway holiday location, as I was a stressed-out teacher at that time. When we were in St Buryan, we would walk the country lanes hand in hand. We got to know many of the villagers on our frequent visits and we would explore the countryside and the coast. Porthcurno, the

Minack Theatre and Lamorna Cove were all nearby and regularly visited. I have lovely memories of us sitting alone on an old wooden bench at the local cricket ground, simply observing nature. We did, of course, still see ourselves as young lovers, although we last did it together when we were well into our late seventies! On sunny days, we would enjoy the beach at Porthcurno, a visit to the Minack up the hill, and a picnic lunch. We soon discovered where to eat out in West Cornwall, with its many hidden gems of pubs and eateries.

Our regular trips to St Buryan continued for many years. Things really got better at the Tower Park site when Jerry and Jude Gibson took over and became the proprietors. We quickly realised that things had improved in many ways. Val and I soon became friends with the couple, and our holidays renting a static caravan continued. It became something that Val and I looked forward to, sometimes twice a year. An easy drive down the A30 from Exeter, stopping for a meal at the Jamaica Inn on Bodmin Moor, then enjoying a week in beautiful West Cornwall.

Through our visits to Tower Park, we were fortunate to meet Jude Gibson's parents, Wendy and Rod Lewis; also her sister, Sarah, and her husband, Ian. These lovely people did much to make our holidays in Cornwall even happier and very memorable occasions. Their friendship and kindness over the years enhanced our holidays in many ways. In what turned out to be Val's last few years, the Gibson and Lewis families contributed much to her happiness. I am very grateful for that and it means a lot to me. I recall particularly memorable visits when Val and I were introduced to Jack, Sarah's newborn son, Wendy and Rod's first grandson. Val was so happy at that time. On another visit, my dear wife made sure she bought the then toddler, Jack, a birthday present. We were privileged to see this young man in the early years of his life, enjoying his family's wonderful campsite, playing on the swings and walking in the wonderful Cornish countryside.

After Val's illness in 2015, when she was in the care home in Teignmouth, these good folk in Cornwall did not forget her. In what I thought were really outstanding gestures of kindness and affection, Val received several beautiful bouquets of flowers from the Scilly Isles, cards to her, plus photos of Jack as he grew up. Val always knew and understood where they had come from and she treasured them. There were always tears from Val, but they were happy tears of joy as we talked together in her room of our happy memories of being together in West Cornwall, at St Buryan.

I recently visited St Michael's Church in Teignmouth on the second anniversary of Val's death. After lighting a candle for Val, I sat by myself in the Lady Chapel, alone with my thoughts. I allowed the memories to flood back into my mind; our many lovely times together in Cornwall returned to me. They were so clear and detailed in my thoughts. It was an uplifting and quite special time for me. I was able to relive, albeit briefly, some of the happiest times in our marriage, and it filled me with joy and pleasure. Although ostensibly it was a sad day for me, it no longer seemed so for a few minutes. Those memories helped me to concentrate on the many,

many good things that we had done together and how remarkable and profound love can be.

If anyone should be, by chance, thinking of a holiday as they read this, look no further than beautiful West Cornwall. We enjoyed outstanding holidays there over many years, often in spring or autumn, outside the main vacation months, especially the small village of St Buryan and Tower Park Camping and Caravan Site.

There are a few memories that often come to mind. Val and I would start a day at Tower Park deciding where we would go that day. After discussing this over breakfast, Val would take a short walk up to the local post office in the village for a daily paper and often to post some cards. We would then set off in the car for Penzance, where we would visit the large Sainsbury's store on the seafront. We would usually enjoy a coffee and a snack in the cafeteria there with its lovely view over Mounts Bay and St Michael's Mount; this would also include enjoying the often sunny sight of the Scillonian ship or other ships and fishing boats making their way out to sea. Then we were off to Porthcurno or Lamorna Bay to spend a day on the beach. On one of the last times Val and I were in Cornwall, she expressed a wish to visit all our favourite spots; Porthcurno, Lamorna Cove and the Minack Theatre among them.

It was as if Val had a premonition about her impending stroke and illness. We enjoyed the visits and I remember vividly that we met a German couple, holidaymakers, that day at the Minack Theatre. This couple were touring Cornwall on a large motorcycle. They were married and much younger than us. As they were admiring the view from the Minack, Val spotted them and she told me that they were speaking in German; she urged me to talk to them. As she was insistent and the place was largely deserted at the time, being autumn, I approached them. Trying to conjure up my best German accent, I was as polite as I could be, enquiring if they were on holiday, and so on. It went surprisingly well and I was amazed how my long-neglected German language came back to me. We had a long chat, all four of us, as Val managed some conversation in German, and we ended up using a strange mixture of English and German. It is well known that most Germans can speak English, of course. It turned out to be an interesting encounter and it enabled us to do our bit to foster Anglo-German relations and promote the wonders of West Cornwall at the same time.

In previous years, we had experienced one or two other interesting encounters while holidaying at Tower Park, St Buryan. When Val was working as a bookseller at Waterstones in Exeter, she mentioned to me that she had met an author who happened to live near St Buryan. It seems that he had invited her to visit him and his wife when we were next in Cornwall. The author was called Derek Tangye, and his wife, Jeannie, was also famous and an author too. I knew that an extra pull and attraction for Val was the fact that this couple had some pet donkeys and Val loved donkeys! Anyhow, the next time we travelled to Cornwall and we were happily installed at Tower Park, Val suggested that we take up Mr Tangye's kind offer. She made the required telephone calls and the following day we set off to find the couple's remote cliff top cottage and smallholding. We had a lovely visit and the couple were charming hosts; Val happily petted the donkeys and cats and helped to feed them with our hosts. It seems that the donkeys and some of the cats were also famous as subjects in Tangye's books. Val knew that but it was a revelation to me. The cottage and smallholding, called Dorminack, was in a splendid isolated area, down a long lane close to Lamorna Cove, with plenty of land and lovely views out to sea.

The coffee and scones morning with the Tangyes led to an even more notable encounter, when Val and I met author John le Carré. He had a coastal cottage close to the Tangyes at Dorminack and he was a friend of theirs, naturally. We were to see quite a lot of le Carré, as he used the small post office in St Buryan. Another charming man, a gentleman. I had long admired and enjoyed his many books and film adaptations. I was in awe of him and virtually struck dumb in his presence; luckily, not so Val, who had all the bookseller's knowledge and expertise to have a good conversation with the great man. Sadly, Mr le Carré died recently, in his eighties.

Val and I really developed our love affair with Scotland on our delayed but wonderful honeymoon in Edinburgh way back in 1958. It was our first visit to the country and where, together, we established an instant love of it and its people. It soon became a favourite holiday destination for us in the UK, which remained with us for more than fifty years. There were some other things that had attracted us to Scotland. My father had been brought up in Perth and lived there until he was twelve years old. I was already well versed in all things Scottish from listening to my father's endless tales and anecdotes from when I was a young child. I certainly grew up knowing quite a lot about fishing on the River Tay and the delights of Scottish delicacies, including single malt whisky.

Throughout our long marriage, Val and I spent many wonderful holidays in Scotland. After our Edinburgh honeymoon, in the following years, we visited some part of Scotland virtually every year. Early in our marriage, at the time of our frugal camping holidays, we spent some extremely unhealthy holidays sleeping in a tent at the Scone Palace Campsite, outside Perth. I remember clearly thick dews and frosty mornings in the Perthshire countryside. Struggling to manage a tiny gas stove in order to brew a hot beverage to sustain us. Wrapped up in many sweaters and clinging to each other, not only out of love but in order to survive! Luckily, these rather spartan holidays did not last long. We graduated to affording the hire of a static caravan on the site; such luxury! Val had always loved caravans and she would produce excellent fried breakfasts and mugs of steaming tea and coffee before we would set off on an early-morning walk around the beautiful countryside, hand in hand and suitably dressed for the cold air.

Over the years, we continued to visit Scotland regularly. The holidays themselves changed but our delight in the location never wavered. We eventually moved on from train trips to Scotland to long car trips from Exeter to Perth. One of these I recall was particularly memorable; it was in the early years. I owned an MGB GT sports car at the time and Val decided we should try to travel to Scotland by road.

"Why not?" she said. "We can stop en route if we want to." I must admit that the prospect quite excited me at the time. Remember, this was the early days of our marriage, when we were holidaying in a tent. I had not realised just how much Val intended to take with us. The tent and essential equipment virtually filled the boot of the car. I had to buy and then fix up a roof rack on the car, and to this was strapped two suitcases and what seemed like everything but the kitchen sink!

When I explained to Val that she would have to leave some things behind, she was not amused. I worried that the car wouldn't be able to cope with all the weight. Some things, like our two sleeping bags, were essential. I explained to Val that they sold food in Scotland, and she reluctantly unloaded some of her food products!

We set off for Scotland. I was carried away over the first few hours by Val's enthusiasm and cheery optimism en route. It was, I can now admit, in retrospect an exciting time in our lives. We were together, we loved each other and we were on an adventure; something unique for us and a challenge. I was nevertheless nervous driving on the motorway. I was worried that the constant rattles from the roof rack indicated the likelihood of us dropping tent poles or suitcases on the very busy motorway! Val was oblivious to my concerns as she sang loudly to the car's radio, which was at full blast throughout the journey.

We reached Preston in Lancashire and I tentatively suggested to Val that we make a stop overnight; I was already shattered. An MGB, even a GT, is not the car for a long road journey. When we stopped in Preston, I had real difficulty in standing up straight again and

I ached all over. Val, a tiny eight-stone, five-foot-tall young woman, was perfectly okay. On the other hand, my twelve-stone, six-foot-plus frame was suffering badly from the journey. We discussed things at length and eventually Val suggested we drive on to Blackpool for the night. Her eyes lit up at the thought so I agreed. After a lengthy discussion, we parked on the seafront in Blackpool, being bombarded by seagulls. We settled on a night's accommodation there.

The following morning, we set off again for Scotland. As we drove along, Val informed me that she had forgotten to pack a washing-up bowl or a bucket. Considering the limited interior of the car was already crammed full, this surprised me! I suggested we stop at lunchtime in Carlisle, get a snack lunch and then perhaps buy the essential bowl and bucket. We did that and it went well. Val found an ironmonger's shop and with some jubilation came back to the car waving a red bucket and bowl at me!

We eventually reached our destination, Perth, and made our way over the River Tay to Scone and our camping site. Scone Palace Camping Site is in a lovely location, situated in the grounds of the palace, alongside Perth Racecourse. It has ample room for tents and a large area for holiday caravans, with some static caravans available for hire. There are toilet blocks with showers and an on-site small shop. The whole place is well maintained and there are many lovely rural walks nearby. When we were there, Val and I often walked for miles in the surrounding woods, down well-worn paths and tracks where the scenery was magnificent and the air always invigorating. In an evening, we would sometimes do a circular walk around the adjoining racecourse; this was quite a novel experience to walk around the steeplechase course. There was the added attraction at certain times of the year of a meeting of the Races, where the racecourse facilities, restaurants, bars, and so on were all available to us, on our doorstep, so to speak.

Back to our first visit. We found a spot for our tent and spent what seemed like hours unloading the car and erecting the tent. We were pleased with ourselves as we surveyed the finished item. The tent was secure, the waterproof groundsheet in place and our sleeping bags spread out, awaiting our first night's sleep. Reality began to hit home as the night drew in. The first thing that hit us was noticing that it was rapidly becoming colder. Our naïve ideas about wearing pyjamas in a tent were quickly dropped; we would keep all our clothes on! That night remains firmly etched in my memory. Val and I laughed about it many times over the following years. We spent the night literally clinging to each other, shivering, but by some miracle sleeping for a few hours, now and then, due to the exhaustion of the trip up to Scotland.

As dawn broke with a wonderful sunrise over the hills, we realised that everything was wet through inside the tent, including us! The very heavy dew had permeated our groundsheet and most other things. I noticed tears welling up in Val's eyes and, to be honest, I felt like joining her in a good cry. Luckily, we did the right thing and with the help of the site's facilities and shop, we had recovered somewhat by ten in the morning. We had hot showers in the site's toilet block, changed all our clothes, did some laundry and enjoyed a large breakfast in the café. We then sat down together to have a conversation on what to do next. It was autumn, October, so really we should have known better about what to expect in Perthshire at that time of year. After some discussion with the site staff, we managed to hire one of the static caravans for the rest of the week. It was with considerable delight that we returned to our tent and began to dismantle it and pack things back into our car.

Our week's holiday turned out to be a real learning curve in many ways. We soon decided that a tent holiday was ideal in Cornwall in spring or summer, but not in Scotland in the autumn. That time of year was necessary due to my teaching job, which gave us a break in mid-October, but Scotland would require a hotel or static caravan in future. That first expedition for us turned out quite well in the end. Val loved it and we enjoyed several lovely day trips by car exploring Scotland's beautiful countryside. We travelled north via the Spittal of Glenshee to Deeside and Balmoral. Val, always a fervent royalist, enjoyed her first visit to the Queen's castle, and I enjoyed visiting a Scottish single-malt distillery!

On subsequent trips to Scotland, virtually every year, we were much better at the organisation; making sure that the accommodation was appropriate, travel convenient and that we were suitably clothed. In later years, we graduated to flying from Exeter to Edinburgh, bus to Waverly train station, train to Perth where I would pick up a pre-arranged hire car from the same garage each year. We usually made sure we pre-booked a static caravan. Val preferred caravans to hotels and she enjoyed the self-catering aspect of it.

Initially, we stayed at the Scone Palace site for many years; we were fond of it and we knew it well. During some of our stays there, we went to Perth Races and mixed with the racing 'toffs', on one occasion having a glass of wine in the top enclosure side by side with the patron of the racecourse, the Duke of Atholl! In later years, we moved further to the north and rented static caravans at the Blair Castle site, north of Pitlochry.

They were all lovely holidays and we then developed a bit of a routine. We would always visit Perth City for a day or two, where we enjoyed shopping, visiting some historic areas or buildings and seeking out some of my late father's childhood stomping grounds. A walk along the Inch in Perth was always part of this, where I would try to conjure up a picture of my father being taught how to fly fish by his father many years ago. Perth was always good for a decent meal too; we got to know the many good pubs and cafés where local produce was the norm, although I couldn't sample the single malts, as I was driving!

As Val was a loyal supporter of the royal family, she insisted on a trip via Blairgowrie, Glenshee and Deeside to Balmoral Castle, and she must have visited it many times over the years. We did several tours of the castle and rode in a pony and trap around the estate, and Val was delighted to see HM The Queen at close quarters on several occasions, notably going to Craithie Church on a Sunday when, under orders from Val, I had risen extra early so that we were in a suitable position outside the small church for a good view of the royal family. Val was fair to me always; I was allowed to organise regular trips for us to the Speyside area, home of some of Scotland's most famous distilleries.

We often walked for miles when out on trips in the Highlands; over the years, I took Val to many historical sites, castles and battlegrounds. Our mutual love of history meant that Val did not need much persuading to set off on some long day trip, often in bad weather, to see some bleak area where one would find a small plaque outlining its historical importance or claim to fame. Having been a History student at university, I must have bored Val to tears on some occasions! I particularly remember taking her to all the sites relevant to the Jacobite Rebellions of 1715 and 1745; we visited Sheriffmuir and Culloden among others. Sterling, Edinburgh and Glencoe were also on our itinerary on various holidays. When visiting Edinburgh, we made sure we visited the National Galleries, the Castle and Holyrood House, and in later years, we followed Ian Rankin's *Rebus* trail.

Val was not only a wonderful wife to me and the love of my life, but she was also a very caring person, a kind Christian lady. This shone through so much when we were on our travels. In Israel, Austria, Malta, Singapore and many other places there are examples, by deeds, of what a wonderful, sensitive person she was. An example comes to mind that occurred during a visit to Scotland in the 1980s. We had already established a routine of staying in static caravans when on holiday in Scotland. Val always loved caravans. Large and luxurious or small and cosy, she loved them all. In Scotland, she would take great pleasure in producing delicious meals from local produce sourced from local shops and even farms. She would insist on a trip to Blairgowrie just to buy the local all-year varieties of fruit and vegetables. That area is renowned for its late-season strawberries, for example. Potatoes and meat had to be locally bought and even bread rolls had to come hot from local bakeries. She became quite an expert on traditional Scottish fare, from morning rolls to haggis and neeps, or swede as we English call them. I was very happy to be the beneficiary of all the culinary skill and as a result I was often reluctant to eat out in cafés and restaurants.

On one holiday in the 1980s, we were in our usual spot at Scone Palace and we decided to take a comparatively short day trip down to Kinross and Loch Leven. Our aim was to enjoy the scenery and visit the remains of the castle on Loch Leven where Mary, Queen of Scots, had been imprisoned at one time. Arriving in Kinross, we parked our hire car and Val said that she wanted to stock up on her bread rolls at the local bakery. Val went off to find the bakery while I wandered around the pleasant small town. We had arranged to meet again at a particular spot in town. After waiting at the agreed place for half an hour or so, I began to worry, as there was no sign of Val. I decided to set off in search of her. When I reached the baker's shop, I was amazed to see Val still inside it. She was in deep conversation with a lady behind the counter. As I entered the shop, Val apologised to me and introduced me to the saleslady she was talking to.

I noticed that Val had several bags of things she had already bought and I began to wonder why she was still there. It turned out that the lady had asked Val where she came from and they had started a lengthy conversation. Typical of Val, it ended up with an exchange of addresses and telephone numbers. It seems that this local shop lady, aged about forty, had never had a proper holiday anywhere in her life. She had a husband and two children, quite young children, had been born in Kinross and had lived there all her life. Val, being Val, had invited the lady and her family to holiday with us in Exeter on a bed-and-breakfast basis at no cost to them. Val had apparently given her a glowing description of the delights of South Devon and guessing that the family were not financially well off, made the offer of a free holiday for them. It was typical of Val and at that time I didn't think we would hear from the Kinross bakery lady ever again. I was wrong.

The following year, I arrived home from my school – I was teaching in Exeter at the time – to an excited Val telling me that she had received a telephone call from the bakery lady in Kinross. It seemed that the lady's husband had got a new job in Kinross and they had bought a small car. She wondered if the previous year's holiday offer was still open. I instinctively knew what Val's reply had been! We were living in quite a large house at the time with two spare bedrooms and two toilets, plus plenty of room. Val was so excited. This married couple with two young children would be making the long journey by road from Scotland to experience their first real holiday, with us in Devon. In the weeks before they were due to arrive, Val busied herself with making preparations; everything was washed, polished and in some cases repainted. She even sent the couple maps and detailed instructions so the journey would go well for them. It certainly did go well. A grateful young family enjoyed a free holiday, regarding accommodation, with us in Exeter. All thanks to a casual meeting in a bakery in Kinross but really thanks to Val, my darling wife. I am sure that family long remembered Val, as well as their first taste of swimming at Dawlish Warren!

Although Val and I both grew up with dogs in our homes, throughout our long marriage we only had cats as our pets. The need for a good mouse-catching cat soon became essential when we moved into our first house back in the fifties. Our first cat, Fluffy, not only cleared our little cottage of mice but she converted Val from being wary of cats to becoming a lover of all feline creatures. After that, we had several other cats over the years and we became attached and very fond of them all. They were great company for Val in the early years when I was in the RAF and away a great deal. Our last cat was called 'Gizmo' and she came to us when we were living in Exeter. In fact, she found us really, because she had a good home several houses away from us down the road, but she had to share it with three other cats. Gizmo discovered that we lived in a larger house with a garden, larger than hers, and that the lady of the house, Val, was home some of the day, unlike her mistress! So she took to visiting Val each day, when she would be fussed over, given various treats and food, together with a nice warm room to snooze in or even the occasional lap.

When we were about to move to our retirement bungalow in Dawlish, Gizmo was still visiting on a daily basis. When the cat jumped into one of Val's suitcases as she was packing, and curled up there, Val decided she would have to talk to the cat's owner about her future. As a result of Val's enquiries, and with the blessing of Gizmo's owner, she was allowed to stay with us. So Gizmo travelled with us when we moved to Dawlish. The cat knew that she was on to a 'good thing' moving in with us; no rival cats, lots of attention and the likelihood of being absolutely spoiled by Val. As a result, she was as good as gold on the car journey from Exeter to Dawlish, slept throughout the journey in a large 'pet box with cushions' and excitedly explored her new home on arrival! Gizmo loved Dawlish, particularly the large rear garden we had with large apple trees to climb. She had eight years with us here in Dawlish, where she had a good life and many adventures. The reason for my digressing into one of our cats, Gizmo, is because her passing away at Christmas 2008, aged fifteen years, prompted another interesting trip for us to Scotland.

Although we tried to be adult about it, losing a well-loved pet is always a sad time. Gizmo had been a great comfort to Val during my battle with cancer in 1997, and at other times. We were both upset when the cat died. She is buried in what is now my rear garden, with a suitable floral memorial over the spot. After her death at Christmas, we were both down in the dumps, unhappy and just wondering what to do next. Remembering that Val was an avid royalist prompted an idea. I suggested we take a short break in Scotland, as we always enjoyed holidays there and it might just ease our current sadness. I booked four days in a middle-range hotel in the centre of Edinburgh and managed to get a Flybe flight from Exeter. Val was happier when I told her that it was all booked and that she would be in Scotland for her birthday on the 21st of January. She had always wanted to visit the Royal Yacht Britannia, which is anchored at Leith, the port of Edinburgh. Now she would fulfil yet another little dream.

It was January and as I had planned the trip to coincide with Val's birthday on the 21st, I made sure that it was on that day that we took a bus out to Leith. It was bitterly cold, frosty but dry, and because it was January there were only a few visitors to the Royal Yacht, mostly Japanese tourists with many cameras! Because there were few visitors, we had a guide to ourselves, and Val took full advantage of that to pepper him with questions and detailed research on the building of the yacht, every item of the kitchens and much else!

She loved it and we had a very happy day, including a good meal out in the night to celebrate her birthday, and we did raise a toast to our late cat, Gizmo. It was a good four days and once again Scotland had come up trumps for us when we needed it, giving us some more lovely memories to treasure. I now often look at some of Val's souvenirs with affection; ornaments, postcards and a guidebook to the Royal Yacht, plus photos of Gizmo the cat sleeping soundly on Val's lap. In the bungalow here now, they are all a constant reminder and give me a warm love-filled glow, to this day.

Chapter 8

On Our Travels – Overseas

Val and I had long harboured dreams of visiting the Holy Land, Israel. We were both interested in the geography, the history and the religious aspects of the region. Val often told me that she didn't know why she had this strange feeling, a fascination with Judaism and the Holy Land. For Val, it probably stemmed from her faith, her love of travel generally, her love of history and her reading. In my case, the interest must to a great extent be in my blood. Having researched my family tree, I discovered a Jewish connection. My maternal grandmother – her maiden name was Kate Marks – came from a Jewish family; my research also showed that on my paternal side, there was a strong Jewish link too. My surname is also a derivation of Soloman after all! If one adds to that my love of history, which I studied at university, it is not surprising that we both had a wish to travel to Israel. In particular, we both wanted to visit the National Israeli Holocaust Memorial at Yad Vashem in Jerusalem; and, of course, to make a pilgrimage to the Christian biblical sites.

In April 1984, we made this dream come true. After much research, many letters and even phone calls to Israel, accommodation in Tel Aviv was secured. It was booked through an Israeli company called Homtel and, although we were somewhat taking a walk into the unknown, and at quite a risk, we made the needed transfer of funds in full payment.

We rented an apartment in Yarkom Street, Tel Aviv, a wealthy area facing the River Yarkom. It was owned by an El Al air stewardess who rented it out through Homtel when she was away on her long-haul flights. I booked our flights from London to Tel Aviv separately, an evening flight, with El Al, the national Israeli carrier. We were aware that April did coincide with Easter and also the Jewish festival of Passover or Pesach, and that Israel would be full of pilgrims and celebrants; Christians and Jews. Unfortunately, we had little choice of days because of the school holidays, the only three weeks that I was free to travel. So we ended up paying premium prices both for air fares and the accommodation. Such considerations meant very little to us, though. The excitement grew steadily as our departure approached. I clearly remember Val perusing various books, guidebooks and maps prior to the trip.

Unbeknown to us at the time, the day of our first-ever trip to Israel was to be a day of some infamy. It turned out to be the weekend of the 1984 Libyan Embassy Siege and the tragic death of a policewoman, Yvonne Fletcher, in London.

Our first flight to Israel was certainly a major learning experience. The level of security at Heathrow for passengers to Israel, particularly El Al passengers, has to be seen to be believed. It is certainly interesting and a little frightening. The extra hours' booking-in time, the segregation at the main terminal and the fact that the flights to Israel never take off on time are all rather unique. The fact that our packed flight also carried two armed air marshals, or security men, was another interesting difference from our usual flights. We took off some half an hour late in an aircraft crowded with mainly Jewish travellers. Val and I, as Anglican Christians, felt somewhat lonely and we clutched each other's hands tightly for more than four hours in the air! We did, it is true, enjoy an excellent meal and several drinks during the flight with the compliments of El Al.

The first we knew about the events that were taking place in London during our flight was a tannoy announcement by the captain as we circled Ben Gurion Airport in Tel Aviv. The pilot gave us a brief summary of the events in London and told us that, as a result, security had been tightened in Israel and in the Middle East generally. It was not the sort of news we wished to hear, as we were already in a state of some unease. As the aircraft made its approach to land, we were suddenly plunged into darkness when all the aircraft's internal lights went off without any warning. We later learned that this was to avoid any missile strike by anti-Israeli Arab terrorists! We were rather happier when we left the plane to climb aboard a large waiting coach, until we noticed three Jeeps full of heavily armed Israeli soldiers, bristling with machine guns, who were to escort us safely to the terminal buildings. Val would not let go of my hand as we both wondered what we had let ourselves in for!

We were even more nervous after we had endured more than forty minutes of intense interrogation by Israeli border officials. They wanted to know why we wished to visit Israel and why we were not staying at a hotel like other visitors. Were we really just simple Christian pilgrims? They kept insisting that I must be Jewish, with a name like Salmon, and somehow they knew about my Jewish family connection through my grandmother, Kate Marks! I was a little annoyed at the attitude and at one time even thought about offering to drop my trousers to prove the point that I was not Jewish! It was quite an experience and not a very pleasant one. One of the officials – they were all armed to the teeth with sidearms – eventually stamped our passports with a visa for entry and smiling at last, wished us a good holiday in Israel. We were both very quiet and subdued as we carried our cases out of the Ben Gurion terminal and went to find a taxi. The taxi driver was an Arab and he was friendly and chatty on the journey to our apartment in Tel Aviv, several miles from the airport at Lod. He was, of course, very unkind and dismissive about Israeli bureaucracy and the police and the way they treated all non-Jewish visitors at the airport.

It was nearly midnight when we arrived at Yarkon Street and our rented apartment. We were greeted by a smartly dressed Israeli complete with *kippa* on his head, who introduced himself to us as the Homtel rental company's rep. He then proceeded to ignore us completely, leaving us standing with our luggage on the pavement, and he started to berate the poor Arab taxi driver in either Hebrew or Arabic! After more than five minutes of verbally lashing the poor taxi driver, he calmly turned, produced a bunch of keys and led us into the luxury flat. While showing us around and giving Val detailed instructions for using the kitchen and washing facilities, he told us that the taxi driver had deliberately taken a long route from the airport to our apartment in order to increase his fare. True or not, it was some introduction for us to life in Israel and Arab-Israeli relations!

After collapsing into the very comfortable double bed in the air-conditioned apartment, Val and I slept soundly until the morning. After a light breakfast and further exploration of the lovely apartment, including its balcony overlooking the river opposite, we decided to start our adventures and explore Tel Aviv for the first time, with some newly engendered excitement.

We spent the first few days exploring the vibrant and very exciting city of Tel Aviv, enjoying coffees at many restaurants and tiny bistros, *falafel* from the many small kiosks and the occasional glass of Israeli wine. It was the start of one of the most fascinating and stimulating holidays that Val and I ever had together in our long and wonderful marriage. We were both excited, happy and very much in love. We shared so much in common and it was a truly memorable period in our lives. The early fears that we had about our safety quickly disappeared. The presence of so many armed soldiers and police was very reassuring. It was strange to see so many female soldiers and police, in equal numbers with their male counterparts. In Israel, both sexes have to do their National Service in the IDF, the Israeli Defence Force. Unusually, in what appears to be a patriarchal society like Judaism, modern Israel seems to have adopted and settled into a system that works for them, with few signs of any sexual discrimination.

This first visit to Israel stands out in my memory now as outstanding for both of us. I am sure that it influenced both Val and I enormously. It had a great bearing on how our future years together were to unfold.

As the days moved on we booked coach trips with very efficient tour guides to all of the famous biblical sites. We visited Tiberias on the Sea of Galilee, Bethlehem, Nazareth, Jerusalem, Jericho and Gethsemane. We spent many hours in places we had both dreamed about as children; the Stations of the Cross in the Old City of Jerusalem, the Church of the Holy Sepulchre, the Church of the Nativity and the Garden Tomb. In two weeks, we managed to also have wonderful days exploring other parts of the country. A fantastic day at the Holocaust Memorial, Yad Vashem; Mea She'arim, the Orthodox Jewish Quarter and a visit to the Israeli Parliament, the Knesset.

We visited Caesarea, via Hadera, and we spent many happy hours exploring the Roman remains. Fascinating hours for me, as I had studied the Roman Empire as part of my education. We tried to cram everything into these fourteen days and we did quite well in ticking off our 'want-to-see' list.

We visited the Hadassah Medical Centre outside Jerusalem, where Val was delighted to be able to stand in front of and admire the famous stained glass windows by Marc Chagall in the centre's synagogue. Yet another wonderful day on this holiday came when we visited the Dome of the Rock and the El-Aqsa Mosque in Jerusalem. Our visit to the River Jordan proved to be a particularly emotional one; to stand where Jesus was baptised by John the Baptist brought tears to Val's eyes. She visited this same spot several times during our five trips to the Holy Land. Significantly, water from the River Jordan was sprinkled on Val's coffin at her funeral; it had been brought here by some church members after a pilgrimage to Israel. More about this in Chapter 11. Two of our specific visits on the holiday deserve some special attention here. One was our first visit to Yad Vashem, the Holocaust Memorial; the other was our day at Masada in the desert.

If Val was crying and very emotional on her visit to the River Jordan, it was nothing to her reaction to our first visit to the Holocaust Memorial at Yad Vashem. We were both very upset by it. It is impossible to make a visit there without being affected deeply in an emotional way. Seeing all the many memorials and displays and reading the facts and figures alone is quite absolutely mind-blowing and hard to accept. To get one's head around the fact that it actually happened and the enormity of it all is a challenge in itself. The most moving display for both of us was the 'Hall of the Children'. As one walks through in semi-darkness, a voice continuously reads the names of the children who were known to have died in concentration camps. Simply walking along looking at the faces of these children in photos, listening to their names and then seeing a huge pile of shoes that were taken from these poor little souls before they were gassed, remains etched in one's memory forever. We both had to sit quietly on a bench and try to compose ourselves after this experience; the tears kept coming, on and off, throughout that day. It became a little easier on subsequent holidays in Israel when we revisited Yad Vashem; but it always brought tears to our eyes. We also saw the memorial plaque to Oskar Schindler of Schindler's Ark/List. He is buried in a Catholic church on the edge of the Old City of Jerusalem.

Our first visit to Masada in 1984 was particularly memorable. Masada is a flat-topped mountain on the southern side of the Dead Sea. It was at Masada that the last group of Jewish Zealots

held out in rebellion against the Romans. The Romans had besieged the Jews there for three years by AD 73. At last, when they were unable to get food and water, the Jews committed mass suicide rather than give in to the Romans. The siege and Masada are revered by today's Israelis. There is an inn, a youth hostel, snack bar and a large restaurant at the foot of the mountain near the cable car station.

The day we visited Masada, it was 100 degrees F! We took the cable car up to see the ruins of the Zealots' settlement at the top of the mountain and we walked down the easier bank path from the 1,450-foot summit.

After a refreshing meal in the restaurant, Val needed to go to the toilet. When she hadn't returned after twenty-five minutes, I went to see where she had got to. There seemed to be a bit of a commotion outside the ladies' toilet, with several heavily armed male soldiers in attendance. It transpired that Val had got herself locked in a cubicle in the toilets and couldn't get out! Her desperate pleas for help eventually resulted in the military arriving. She was rescued by a very handsome Israeli soldier, complete with AK45 rifle over his shoulder, climbing over the cubicle and releasing the jammed lock. I remember vividly seeing my darling wife emerging from the ladies' toilets, clinging to and literally in the arms of a six-foot plus, tanned and very handsome Israeli soldier. She was upset, of course, but I am certain she was just a little bit reluctant to release her hold on the muscular Adonis who had rescued her. It became a fond memory over the years of our marriage; I often teased Val about the incident at Masada, suggesting to her that the attractions of Israeli soldiers had something to do with it.

On our fourth visit to the Holy Land in August 1992, Val and I stayed at the Anglican Christ Church Hospice in the Old City of Jerusalem. This is a very old hospice and church situated just inside the walls of the Old City, by the Jaffa Gate. The accommodation was rather spartan but clean and welcoming. We had a rather plain double bedroom with en-suite facilities, and we took meals in a large well-appointed dining room. We soon made friends with some of the other Christian English visitors who, unlike us, were on their first pilgrimage to the Holy Land. They were all ladies and Val was very popular with them when she offered to show them some of the sights of the Old City. They jumped at the offer, as it saved them paying a local guide. I was left at the hospice when they went off one morning. I enjoyed the time alone, reading and sunbathing in the lovely gardens. On another day, the ladies thanked Val by inviting her to join them on a taxi tour trip into the Palestinian West Bank, which she enjoyed telling me about in some detail on her return.

We decided one day to make a second visit to another hospice, St Andrew's, which stands on a hill overlooking the Hinnon Valley and the Old City. This is a Church of Scotland hospice and memorial church which we had previously visited in 1989 when we were staying in the seaside town of Netanya. On that day, it was a brief visit because we had made quite a long journey from Netanya by train via Tel Aviv. So we set off early in the morning after our breakfast at Christ Church. We had decided to walk to St Andrew's, unlike most visitors, who seemed to take taxis everywhere. We were happy to walk, knowing it was quite safe to do so. The only problem for us was the sun as we walked along the busy roads. It was August after all. We were both suitably dressed, including light clothes, large hats and sunglasses. On our arrival at St Andrew's, we were quickly given large ice-cold drinks, which we enjoyed at a table in their gardens. To our left was the British Consul building with a Union Jack flying, in contrast to the Saltire fluttering over St Andrew's. There was a lovely view as we enjoyed our refreshment. One could see over the Hinnon Valley to the Old City of Jerusalem bathed in sunshine. On that day, Val and I met the Minister of St Andrew's, the Rev. Colin Morton. Over coffee, he introduced us to Mrs Margaret Crawford, head teacher of the Church of Scotland Tabeetha School in Jaffa, Tel Aviv. This church foundation school uses English as its language of instruction and aims to teach children of all faiths together, side by side; Christians, Jews and Muslims. The Israeli State is not keen on this! As a result, many obstacles, a lack of cooperation, bureaucracy, and so on mean that the school does not find funding or support easy. Many poor children, Muslim in particular, suffered.

As I was a teacher at the time, Mrs Crawford invited us to visit her school the following day. We got to the school the next day, having taken the train from Jerusalem to Tel Aviv and a taxi to the school in Yafet Street, Jaffa. Val was very upset on seeing the school's lack of teaching resources. Books were in short supply, both in the primary and secondary sectors. Val was determined to help them. On our return to the UK, she made sure that I gathered support from my school and my contacts in education. We collected old and spare textbooks, and also money via donations from friends and colleagues, to buy some new books. We shipped parcels of old primary readers, new physics books and anything that was useful to a poor school in Israel.

Carriage costs, customs procedures and other barriers were put in our way, but Val, being Val, made sure that Tabeetha School pupils got a better deal. On a subsequent visit to the Holy Land in 1994, we stayed at St Andrew's Hospice in Jerusalem again and we managed to pack our luggage with a few more new and much-needed textbooks for Tabeetha School. It was very difficult but interesting explaining to the Israeli authorities at Ben Gurion Airport what we were up to. We kept in touch with Tabeetha School for many years after that, although we were not able, unfortunately, to visit Israel again after 1994. Val often talked of going to Israel again, even in her late seventies. It was certainly a special place for both of us and this was remembered at Val's funeral in 2019.

Although Val professed not to be a great football fan, being married to me meant that she would inevitably acquire some interest in the beautiful game. As a result, whenever she was asked who her favourite team were, she would always reply Liverpool. This naturally outshone my answer, which would be the very humble Exeter City! Why should I bring up the subject of football in a chapter entitled *On Our Travels – Overseas*? Let me explain.

In May 1988, Val and I planned our second eagerly awaited trip to Israel. We booked two weeks at an apartment in Netanya, a coastal resort just north of Tel Aviv. We made the booking through Homtel Ltd., the Israeli company we had used for our first adventure to the Holy Land in April 1984. The accommodation consisted of a first-floor luxury apartment in the wealthy outskirts of the small Mediterranean resort, complete with balcony and upmarket furnishings. We had been very happy with Homtel's apartment in Tel Aviv four years earlier and equally happy with the booking arrangements, payment methods, paperwork, and so on. We felt that we could trust them implicitly. As I was happy with our booking arrangements, I went ahead and booked two tickets with

El Al, the Israeli national airline, Heathrow to Tel Aviv, return.

We were already familiar with the extra hassle of any flight to Israel from our 1984 trip. The fact that one had a much longer waiting period between booking in at the airport and taking off, the understandable extra security and the completely separate pre-flight waiting area with its own restaurant, shops and facilities. Once in this 'Israel Only' area, one could not leave it, and one was only mixing with passengers for Tel Aviv or passengers coming in from Tel Aviv. So here we were once again, sitting in a very comfortable part of this large secure area with hand baggage only, drinking endless coffees and eating snacks. It was an evening flight. As usual, Val decided to go to the toilet. I knew this would involve her wandering around the large area and having a look at our fellow passengers on the flight! I was not unduly worried when she had not returned after half an hour or so! When she eventually returned and sat down beside me, I did notice that she did seem a little excited.

"I've been talking to someone famous," she said. She waited for me to respond and I deliberately took my time. Eventually, I deigned to ask her who it was. "Bob Paisley," she said. "The former Liverpool manager." Being quite a football fanatic at the time, this quickly got my attention. She then told me that he was sitting a short distance away from us, waiting for the same flight as we were. She went on to tell me how charming he had been to her when she had approached him, ostensibly for an autograph. He invited her to sit with him for a coffee and they had chatted for a while.

"You can go up and meet him," she then told me. She explained that she had told Mr Paisley that her husband was 'mad on football', and he had invited me to join him in the lounge area where he was. I was off in a flash! I shook hands with the Liverpool football icon and listened as he told me why he was travelling to Israel. I meanwhile gabbled on about Liverpool FC, Shankly and many very famous Liverpool players. I certainly knew that Bob Paisley was an even more successful manager of Liverpool than Bill Shankly, between 1974 and 1983, in domestic football and European football. He had retired when we met, of course, and he told me that he had been invited to Israel to advise their football chiefs on improving their International team and developing their leagues in Israel. Although he was going as an adviser on football matters, he was an official guest of the President of Israel, Chaim Herzog. The President was born in Ireland and was a football fan himself, so he was naturally drawn to Liverpool! I enjoyed our chat and thanked him profusely for not only making my day, but also my wife's! He was a real gentleman and charming to talk to.

When we did eventually get on the aircraft we did not see Bob Paisley, as he was already on board in the first-class or 'King David-class' section. However, halfway through our flight, he came back through the aircraft and found us in our tourist-class seats, especially to wish us well on our holiday. Quite a charming gesture by a real gentleman. On landing at Ben Gurion Airport in Tel Aviv, we spotted Mr Paisley again. He was being ushered through as a VIP. He again acknowledged us with a friendly wave, which was very kind of him, as he was directed out and into the President of Israel's huge limousine, with flag and police motorcycle escort!

As a postscript here, Val seemed to have a habit of meeting famous people in the football world. She was visiting London on a day trip from Exeter with her friend Phyllis Chudley when she quite literally bumped into Bobby Charlton. They were in a crowded Harrods store when this man in a beautiful camel-haired overcoat turned quickly and managed to knock tiny Val over! He helped her up with many apologies, with Val evidently spluttering, "It's okay, Mr Charlton, I'm not hurt." On that occasion, she did not get an autograph.

Phyllis Chudley, the lady who was with Val on that day in London, was an ex-bookseller colleague of Val's. The same lady's brother, John Bradbury, and his wife were the couple we spent our silver wedding with in Toronto, Canada, in 1982 (see earlier chapter).

Between 1984 and 1994, we made five visits to the Holy Land, Israel; they were all very special for us. There are so many memories of those holidays that it is difficult to choose what to include in this book and what to leave out. I have three large photo albums dedicated to those five trips, and I often spend many hours looking at them. I find it easy to conjure up clear and detailed recollections of events and places, and sometimes even humorous occasions, from those trips.

One particularly interesting memory from our five visits to Israel is certainly noteworthy; I refer to our involvement with the Israeli Secret Service, commonly known as the Mossad. I have mentioned elsewhere the strict and very thorough interrogation that all non-Jewish visitors to Israel undergo at airports. This has to be experienced to be believed. It was certainly a revelation to us on each of our trips. The questions, the probing and the suspicion blatantly shown by well-armed officials of both sexes were quite frightening and even threatening at times. Nevertheless, after our first trip, we got used to it to some degree. The involvement of the 'other', i.e. Secret Services, was quite different.

Our earliest acquaintance with the undercover agents happened during our first trip to Israel in April 1984. We were staying in a rented apartment in Tel Aviv. This itself caused some concern during our interrogation at Ben Gurion Airport, when the security people could not understand why a Christian couple on their first trip on holiday to Israel should have accommodation in a private apartment. "Why are you not staying in a hotel like other visitors?" This was a question repeated in several forms.

A few days into the holiday, we were out shopping in the fashionable Dizengoff Street of Tel Aviv when we got the distinct impression that we were being watched closely. Val agreed with me that two smartly dressed men seemed to be paying us a lot of attention. They even turned up in several of the large stores we had entered. Like a script from a Hollywood movie, we deliberately tried 'to lose our tails' and we thought we had been successful after half an hour, when they seemed to have disappeared. Feeling happy and wondering if we had imagined it all, we wandered back down Dizengoff's wide street. We stopped for a moment, deciding whether to visit the British Airways office to check on our El Al return flight to London. Suddenly we were approached by the same two young men, who appeared from nowhere. They both smiled beautifully and were most polite to us.

"Can we help you?" one of them said. "You look lost."

Their English was impeccable. I muttered something about the fact that we were looking for the British Airways office.

"It's just over there," one of them said, pointing up the street; and with that, they wandered off. Their last words were "Have a good day." Val and I were, to say the least, a little disturbed. Later, when back in our apartment, we agreed that we had certainly been watched and were under some sort of surveillance. The two young men had been wearing suits, unusual in Israel, although they were lightweight. They had looked the epitome of American FBI agents, as seen in films.

Our second similar experience occurred in 1988, when we were staying in the coastal resort of Netanya. Once again, we had rented a private apartment in a wealthy area of Netanya. Our first-floor accommodation overlooked a wide tree-lined street, and was complete with its own balcony. Each morning, Val would prepare breakfast, which we would eat out on the balcony with the Mediterranean sun beating down on us, which necessitated the wearing of floppy hats and good sunglasses. We could see all movements up and down the street and we commented on the peace and tranquillity of the area. There were a few cars from time to time but little sign of pedestrians. After a few days, we noticed that one car, a large Volvo estate, seemed to be on view every day. It was parked in a strange and different place on the road each day but was always close to our block of flats. We also noticed that this car had an abnormally large number of radio aerials sticking up at its rear. Given our previous experience from our 1984 visit to Tel Aviv, we became a little nervous about the car being there every day. During our observations each morning, we rarely saw any driver. We decided to try to ignore this during the holiday and simply enjoy the lovely sandy beaches, the good restaurants and the many things to do in the seaside town.

A few days before we were due to leave Israel, we decided to visit the Holy City of Jerusalem by train, via Tel Aviv. It was a journey that we had done before and we had a lovely day in Jerusalem. Tired but happy from revisiting some of our favourite places, including the National Holocaust Memorial at Yad Vashem, we embarked on the return journey to Netanya. When the train pulled into the small station on the outskirts of Netanya, we were amazed to see one car parked outside: the same Volvo estate, complete with radio aerials. As we walked past the car, its door opened and a tall middle-aged man got out and literally stood there and confronted us. He was smartly dressed with slightly greying hair.

"Are you going back into town?" he said.

Taken aback and quite shocked, we were both speechless for a moment. Finding my tongue, I found myself telling him that we were renting an apartment in the town. He asked for the address and I told him. Val just stood there, looking quite troubled and understandably nervous. Without further word, he opened the rear door of the car and ushered us into it, muttering something about it being quite a long journey and he happened to be going that way. We set off up the road away from the station. I looked at Val and she shrugged her shoulders. She still looked nervous and this was confirmed by the way she tightly gripped my hand. Throughout the twenty-minute journey, the man seemed friendly enough, asking where we had come from and what we thought of Netanya as a resort, and he asked about the famous sites we had visited in Israel. His manner was certainly very friendly. We both thought it was quite a strange occurrence and that this man was a 'well-trained operative', whoever he worked for.

Arriving outside our block of apartments, he was ultra-polite in helping Val from the car and he made a point of shaking hands with me and wished us both *bon voyage*. We simply stood there in the road staring after the car as it sped away and vanished around a corner.

Strangely, we did not talk about the incident at all when back in our smart apartment. Instead, we busied ourselves unpacking our bags and talking about where we had been and what we had seen on the day in Jerusalem. It was as if we didn't want to face up to the fact that we both knew that something strange was going on. Later, after Val had prepared an excellent meal, as usual, we settled down on the balcony with large glasses of wine. It was then that we talked about it. We both agreed that we were under some sort of surveillance. Too many strange things had happened on each of our visits to Israel; put together with the very intensive questioning on each arrival and departure at Ben Gurion Airport plus on one occasion rather intrusive questions at a bank in Tel Aviv and we had good reason to be suspicious. If we had any doubts about the surveillance, these were dispelled eventually by the events of 1992.

In 1989, we visited Netanya again, this time during the long school break in August. Although Israel was very hot during this month, we saw it as a change of our routine. To be quite honest, there were other reasons. We managed to buy some bargain British Airways flight tickets; we both felt we needed to recharge our batteries and our favourite destination was the Holy Land. We booked a week in a modest hotel in Netanya and the second week in a better-class four star hotel in Tel Aviv. There turned out to be a marked difference between the two. The one in the resort of Netanya was not very large, although it did have all the basics. It was clean and well run. We had booked a double bedroom which came with a kitchenette and en-suite bathroom, so it really doubled as a small apartment and it suited us at this time. The much larger Tel Aviv hotel for the second week was more upmarket and in the 'hotel area'. Our bedroom was a typical Israeli hotel room, well appointed, bordering on the luxurious, complete with a large en-suite bathroom which was filled with multiple perfumed soaps and every toilet extra one could possibly need, a large drinks bar in the bedroom and truly immaculate décor. Unlike our experience in the small Netanya hotel, where we could cook if we wanted to, the staff at the Tel Aviv hotel would have had a blue fit if we had even tried to eat in their hotel rooms!

Regarding the attention the Mossad had given us during our visits in 1984 and 1988, their attention was conspicuous by its absence in August 1989, both in Netanya and Tel Aviv. There is a simple explanation. On this occasion, we stayed in Israel for two weeks but we were in hotels all of the time. On our previous two visits to Israel, we were in private apartments, booked by ourselves. Hotels in Israel, like many other countries, have strict regulations to follow at all times. The many members of staff, particularly in the larger hotels, that one sees all day ostensibly going about their various duties must include a sprinkling of state agents among their number. A constant flow of information on the activities of foreign guests is easy for an organisation like the Mossad to acquire and to keep up to date with.

When we next visited Israel in the month of August 1992, we again came into contact with the Israeli Secret Service. This time was also a first for us. We decided to spend two weeks in the Holy City itself, Jerusalem. I have already written about this visit earlier, when we met Margaret Crawford, head teacher of Tabeetha School, Jaffa, and our involvement in supporting them. One thing that I did not mention earlier is very relevant to my writing here, namely Val and John meet the Mossad again!

It was towards the end of our stay at the Christ Church Hospice in Jerusalem when we were enjoying a morning cold drink in the gardens, together with Val's English lady friends. Suddenly, as if out of nowhere, a young man approached our garden table. He was tall, handsome and he looked extremely fit. As the only man sitting there, I immediately noticed that all the ladies were immediately focused on this handsome stranger, including Val, I might add. He smiled at us and introduced himself as Jack and asked if he could join our table for a cold drink, which he did. He was charm personified. I was immediately quite suspicious and not a little jealous of this chap's ability to take over the company that I had been enjoying of four ladies, one of whom was my wife. It was as if a world-renowned Hollywood heartthrob star had, by accident, stumbled into the garden of the Christ Church Hospice in Jerusalem.

For nearly three quarters of an hour he sat with us, dominating the conversation in impeccable English as he made the ladies laugh, and he was the absolute centre of attention. What he did not do, however, was to really say much about himself. He hinted that he was something to do with the Israeli military and that he had also served in the UK Royal Marines at one time. He was very good at fielding questions that he didn't want to answer, usually with a light anecdote of his own. After a while, Val did give me a knowing look, which told me that she thought this Adonis was too good to be true. I agreed. He left us eventually, saying that he was travelling down to Eliat, the Israeli resort on the Red Sea. Quite a discussion took place after he had left; over cold drinks, the ladies and myself spent some time discussing the pros and cons of this unexpected event. The three ladies were excited and happy; Val and I were just a little worried that there was a connection with our earlier experiences in Israel. How right we were! In the autumn of 1992, we were to discover that our suspicions about Jack from the Christ Church garden incident were correct.

We were back home in Exeter, at 97 Bonhay Road, that autumn. I was teaching at a secondary school in Somerset, commuting daily, and Val was busy selling books for Waterstones. It was a Saturday morning in early October and Val and I were enjoying our weekend off. We were happy being together as always and quite relaxed. Suddenly our front doorbell rang several times. Thinking this was either a neighbour or travelling salesman, or perhaps a charity collector, I slowly made my way to the front door. When I opened the front door, I was absolutely shocked and amazed at what confronted me. A young couple stood there smiling, and the young man was Jack, whom we had met briefly in the garden of the Christ Church Hospice in Jerusalem some two months before. He quickly said, "Do you remember me? We met in Jerusalem. This is my girlfriend, Ingrid, she's Swedish. We were in Devon so we thought we'd look you up."

To say that I was in shock is an understatement. I found myself automatically ushering the couple in and offering them a seat in our lounge; I was acting like a robot. By this time, Val had joined us and Jack was doing the right thing in introducing the stunning blonde Ingrid to her. Val and I exchanged glances, which said it all. I knew we were both thinking the same things. How did this come about? How did he or they know our address? There were many thoughts racing through our heads at that time. Val, always the polite host, made us all coffees then produced biscuits and slices of her homemade cake, as we all sat down in the lounge.

Friendly and smiling throughout, Jack told us that he did his Royal Marine training at Lympstone, so he knew

Exeter and the area well. He was quite expert at changing the conversation at a moment's notice, at avoiding our rather pointed or awkward questions and managing to continue with trivial chat. His strikingly beautiful companion, Ingrid, let Jack do most of the talking. She concentrated on talking to Val about domestic things, cookers, washing machines and household matters. She even wanted Val to show her around the house and was very kind about Val's décor, curtains, ornaments and the paintings on display in various rooms. There were lots of searching questions from them, however. Why did we visit Israel so often? What did we both think about the Arab/Israeli situation, the conflict? These questions were slipped in between general talk about places of interest in the Holy Land and general topical matters.

The couple managed to stay for more than an hour and not tell us very much about themselves. Val and I were still too shocked and, to be honest, a little afraid to demand answers from them. The young man, Jack, decided when they would leave. He was obviously in charge! They shook hands with us and Jack gave Val a big hug and kiss on the cheek in the Continental style, which did mean that I could enjoy a similar experience with his gorgeous partner! We ushered them out of our front door and the last word that Jack said to me was in Hebrew, *lehitraot*, which I knew was a friendly greeting meaning *see you again soon,* somewhat like the French *à bientôt.*

As you can imagine, Val and I spent an hour or so after they had left talking about what had happened. We both agreed it was a Mossad operation once again.

But this time we were at home, in England. During the time the couple were in our house, there were many indications or clues. They knew where we had stayed on our holidays in Israel; they knew about our visit to Tabeetha School in Jaffa; and they also knew that my maternal grandmother was from a Jewish family. The obvious question was, how did they get all this information, including our address?

We talked about it for most of the weekend and we never forgot it over the years. We did make one more trip to Israel in October 1994. We wondered what sort of reception we would get that time, but our trepidation and fears were unwarranted. We stayed at the Church of Scotland Hospice in Jerusalem, St Andrew's, and we had a great holiday. There was no sign of any surveillance or overmuch attention; we seemed to be left alone. We reckoned that Jack and his Ingrid must have filed a favourable report: Valerie and John Salmon were not enemies or a threat to the State of Israel!

Many years later, Val and I talked about our Israeli adventures and we tried to find reasons for the Mossad's interest in us. The only things we came up with were rather nebulous, to say the least. We had what was accepted in the Middle East as a Jewish surname; my grandmother's family were Jewish; we stayed in private accommodation, not in hotels, on the first three holidays; we supported Tabeetha School, a multi-faith school opposed by the Jewish State; and the most unlikely of all were the facts that Valerie had been an active member of the Labour Party in her teens and that I had been a member of the rather militant National Union of Schoolmasters!

From the late eighties to about 2005, we established a pattern in our holiday destinations, visiting Cornwall and Scotland regularly for the occasional weekend in Cornwall, and a week or more in Scotland. In Cornwall, after our old caravan reached its sell-buy date, we resorted to hiring a static caravan on the same site, Tower Park in St Buryan. We were always happy there and extremely well looked-after by the new proprietors, Jerry and Jude Gibson, with whom we quickly built up a lasting friendship over the years. Jude's parents, Wendy and Rod Lewis, eventually retired to Cornwall and were very involved in running the campsite. These lovely kind people will inevitably feature in other chapters in this book, including the last chapter at the end of Val's life. We did buy a luxury caravan at Tower Park ourselves eventually, and I am sure there will be more about that in the last chapter.

The other UK destination that featured regularly in our holiday plans each year was Scotland. There we graduated from our delayed honeymoon to the first road trip with a tent as accommodation, already described in some detail elsewhere, to trips which involved flying from Exeter to Edinburgh via Flybe airlines and then renting a car in Perth and travelling north to the Highlands.

During this period of our marriage, our overseas holidays also seemed to develop a routine of their own. Each year we would plan at least two overseas holidays. These mainly became regular trips to two countries that we were both very fond of: France and Austria. It helped our choice that we both spoke a passable version of the two languages, French and German. Val was better at

French, I was better at German, helped by the fact that I had lived in Germany for more than two years courtesy of the RAF, when a single man, I should add!

Early in our marriage, we had visited France quite a lot. Our very first overseas holiday together was in Paris and this was followed by trips to Normandy, where we visited and stayed in Arromanches and explored D-Day museums and beaches. We also visited World War One sites in France and Belgium, Brittany on several occasions and had one memorable visit to Lisieux. Our choice of France in the early days of our travel was influenced by several things: easy accessibility by boat and train, by air and even hovercraft, a mutual love of history and the arts and the fact, as mentioned above, that we both spoke French at a level to 'get by'. I must add here that Val's French accent was superb, and with her dress flair and her often very Gallic hairstyle, including a chignon and various French rolls, she was more than once mistaken for a Frenchwoman! As you can imagine, I secretly loved that when in France. Perhaps I should also mention here that Val could sing the French National Anthem, the Marseillaise, all verses fluently in French; a fact that will come up again in the last chapter of this book.

During the nineties, Val made the acquaintance of a lady of some means who owned an apartment in Antibes, a city on the French Côte d'Azur, the South of France's premier holiday area. How she met this lady is a bit of a mystery to me even now. I do know that it was something to do with a magazine that Val subscribed to, *The Lady*, and some correspondence the two of them had over something or other! Anyhow, the two of them became friends and I do myself remember speaking to her on occasion by telephone and taking a message for Val.

Anyhow, as a result of this friendship of Val's, we were offered the opportunity to rent the apartment in Antibes at a very reasonable cost when it was free of the owner's occupancy. The lady herself was a widow and I believe the apartment had been bought by her husband as a present for her; some present!

We made our first arrangements to travel to Antibes with some trepidation but also with some excitement. After all, we were flying out to the holiday area of film stars and millionaires, to our own rented apartment. We had a smooth flight from Heathrow to Nice via BA, and because it was all new to us, we decided to be extravagant and lash out on a taxi from Nice Airport to Antibes. The apartment was beyond our expectations, with a luxury feel about it. It was well furnished, with many electrical gadgets, lifts and telephones. It was also located in an expensive area of Antibes, just back from the seafront in the Rue de Provence.

To say that we were delighted as we sat together on the flat's balcony sipping evening glasses of wine in a still sunsoaked South of France would be an understatement! The following seven days were spent exploring Antibes, swimming off a pristine soft-sand beach and travelling along the famous coastline railway to nearby Cannes, Nice and Monte Carlo. The fact that we were able to visit this lovely area of France regularly over the following six years, staying in a really pleasant apartment with all modern facilities, was quite wonderful. During our holidays there, in Antibes, we visited Cannes and Monte Carlo quite often; we travelled on into Italy for a day trip to Ventimiglia and visited the famous Picasso Museum in Antibes itself. I can understand how Pablo Picasso loved the area so much and did some of his greatest work there; the colours on the coast and inland in Provence are quite out of this world. We also sometimes took a bus trip inland from Haute-Alpes to Provence, exploring small villages and the scent capital of Grasse. Val would cook delicious meals for us each evening in the apartment, having bought local produce. There was plenty of wine, of course, to add to the French ambience! As she did in Scotland, Val always wanted to use the local meat and vegetables in her cooking. It was a great delight for me to watch Val bargain with staff in shops over the price or quality of vegetables or fruit. It was all done in French and she more than held her own, often triumphantly walking away with what she perceived as a bargain. More than once on our visits to Antibes, I thought that Val would be at home there; she seemed so happy and quite content.

There was one thing that Val always insisted on doing when we were in Antibes; throughout six or seven years of holidaying in the same apartment there, she had one thing we always did. Val made sure that when visiting Cannes, we had to walk along the Croisette to the marina where all the luxury yachts were anchored. We had to stroll around there and sometimes sit for an hour or so on a seat. This was particularly so when it was close to the time for the famous Film Festival. The motive behind Val's affinity to Cannes and its large marina was that she hoped to catch a glimpse of Clint Eastwood! She had read somewhere that the film star always stayed on a yacht anchored in Cannes Marina and she was determined to see him. She confessed to me that Eastwood was the only man she would consider leaving me for, even after I had pointed out that he was not available! I have to report that she never saw him there, although there is a postscript to this obsession of Val's with film stars. On one occasion, we were flying back to the UK from Nice after ten days in the apartment in Antibes, when Val made a trip forward on our plane to the toilet. She had to go through the first-class section of the BA plane. When she returned to her seat and to me, she said, "We'll be safe on this trip."

"Why?" I enquired.

"Because James Bond is sitting up there in first class," said Val. She went on to explain that Roger Moore was there, travelling on our plane. I naturally checked for myself in due course, making a visit to the forward toilet. She was right. I remember that I was particularly annoyed when on arrival at Heathrow, Roger Moore got priority treatment recovering his six or seven cases, which he didn't lift or touch, and his handlers/bodyguards did everything for him. I wouldn't argue with Moore himself, though. Although I am six feet tall, he seemed to dwarf me when I was close to him!

The fact that we loved visiting France so regularly, in particular, the Côte D'Azur region, prompted us at one time to consider the possibility of buying a flat there ourselves. We even visited an estate agent's office in Antibes and made some enquiries one time on a holiday.

We even talked about taking up some form of permanent residence '*en France*' too. I clearly remember Val and I having a chat about this idea with one of Val's cousins and her husband.

Cheryl and Andy Walker have a married daughter who lives in the South of France, and they make frequent visits to see their daughter and grandchildren. We had several chats with Cheryl, Val's cousin, and Andy about our common interest and liking for that part of France, and our ideas about moving there. As it turned out, we decided against it on several counts, not least because it would mean leaving family ties behind and also because, at heart, we were both very British! An inherent suspicion of the French came to mind at the time, I remember. Having been a student of History at university, I was only too aware that the '*entente cordiale*' is a modern invention, and I'm prone to remembering the Hundred Years' War and World War II instead!

One of the European countries that regularly featured on our list of holiday destinations was Austria. In Chapter 5, I briefly mentioned our very first holiday in Austria when we stayed in Kitzbühel, a famous ski resort in the Tyrol region. This particular holiday deserves a bit more attention. It was not only a lovely holiday in itself but it also planted the seeds of a lifelong affection that we had for Austria, its people, its food and its music.

The two weeks in Kitzbühel took place when I was still in the RAF, although in my last year of service, in 1967. It was a Thomas Cook special offer and reasonably priced as such. In those days, there were no easyJet cheap flights. A journey from Exeter to Austria entailed a lot of train travel, both in the UK and on the Continent, plus a Channel crossing from Dover to Calais. Throughout this long journey, one had to struggle with heavy suitcases, provide for one's own meals and refreshments, plus suffer many officials demanding to see passports and tickets, almost hourly! To be fair, Cook did their best to help us en route. A man in a peaked cap with a Thomas Cook logo met us at Victoria Station in London and escorted us to our first-class carriage on the boat-train to Dover. He kept an eye on us during the train journey to Dover, and I noted he was nowhere to be seen when we were struggling with our luggage to get on the boat! He miraculously turned up again when Val and I were sitting comfortably sipping drinks in the first-class lounge of the French-owned ferry. He was, however, an interesting companion for the crossing. He regaled Val and I with many tales and also gratefully knocked back all the cognacs that I bought him! He did make sure that we found our reserved seats on the Alpine Express train at Calais and we were pleased about that.

Having said farewell to the Thomas Cook rep, we settled back and enjoyed the long journey to Innsbruck by train. Unlike today, we had to endure passport checks as we travelled across Europe, plus many ticket inspections. The good thing was that there were ample opportunities for refreshment on the train, plus a restaurant car. It was a wonderful opportunity to observe the countryside via the train's windows; an ever-changing panorama of big cities, rural areas and some beautiful scenery. We were glad that our train trip was first class because it ensured that we were not in a crowded compartment and we had the benefits of good facilities on the journey. I think Val enjoyed being treated like a lady by the many officials. In those days, travelling first class was really worth the extra cost.

One little incident comes to mind concerning this train trip from Calais to Innsbruck. We had been enjoying the ever-changing scenery when, as we pulled into the station at Zurich, an announcement told us that we would have a long stop there, so I decided that I would get off the train and stretch my legs on the platform. Val was more cautious; she remained on the train watching me from the corridor window. I decided to stroll along the large, wide platform and to buy two coffees from a stand, to give Val a treat. The inevitable disaster happened when our train whistle blew and railway officials with flags began to wave them! Running along the platform with two hot cups of coffee in order to reach an opened train door, held by an anxious official, was not easy! I made it, but with very little coffee left in the cups and quite badly scalded hands. Val must have reminded me more than a dozen times over the years about my 'Zurich Coffee Moment', and it remains imprinted in my own travel memories.

We reached Innsbruck safely, where we were met by a handsome, suited young man, again courtesy of Thomas Cook, who guided us to a small local train which took us through lovely valleys and mountains, through Westendorf to Kitzbühel. A taxi was waiting for us to take us to our hotel, the Sweitzerhof. Two weeks of excellent food, mountain climbing, sightseeing and generally being spoilt followed. This included our first trip to Salzburg and to the Kufstein Organ in nearby Bavaria, an organ played by Albert Schweitzer many times. Val loved the musical connections in the area; from *The Sound of Music* film sites to Mozart's birthplace and some glorious church music. Attending a nightclub in Kitzbühel was another memorable occasion from this holiday. I often enjoy looking at our many photographs and even 8mm movies of this holiday today. It is true to say that we both fell in love with Austria on that first holiday there and I have fond memories even today of it. Throughout our long marriage, we always tried to include a visit to Austria in our holiday plans.

During the 1970s and the early 1980s, we had several enjoyable holidays in Austria. We visited Fuschl am See, St Gilgen and Salzburg at various times and had lovely holidays each time. We were never disappointed when we chose Österreich as our destination. The Tyrolean scenery with its many mountains and lakes provided us with many long walks, hikes and some mountain adventures. We usually took some 8mm movie film and many 35mm photos at that time. Today, I can enjoy some wonderful memories via the many films and photos that I still have. I have had the movie films transferred to modern DVD format, and I recently watched Val enjoying herself at a mountaintop café in the Tyrol and also writing postcards in the garden of our hotel. Lovely memories.

Later in our marriage, when we were in our sixties and seventies, going to Austria was much easier. We would take a flight from Exeter Airport direct to Innsbruck and travel on to a small local resort, such as Igls, by coach. The fact that I could speak German reasonably well always helped on Austrian holidays, of course. That was thanks to the two years I spent living in Germany with the RAF many years ago! Val was very good too; she made a point of learning some basic German and she would often surprise me when we were in the company of Austrians, by joining in the conversations. My German language skills also became useful if not essential on our holidays in the two big cities of Berlin and Vienna. We both loved Vienna, in particular, for its history and music. We holidayed in Berlin but more frequently in Vienna. We made some great visits to the old Hapsburg capital, sometimes to visit Christmas markets but at other times of the year too. I remember we arrived in Vienna for one holiday and it was pouring with rain as we left the airport. It was a typical mountain thunderstorm, and having got a taxi to the centre of Vienna, Val asked me why I was not wearing a hat. I explained that I had forgotten to pack one. She then proceeded to march me into a very expensive-looking shop of outfitters in the centre of Vienna, where she bought me an expensive German-made waterproof hat. I still have it here, for rainy days! Talking about Vienna, we also made, as mentioned above, several trips in December, over the years, to enjoy the lovely Christmas markets there. I have some really lovely handmade Christmas baubles and decorations which we bought there. They remind me of lovely days, with Val and me sipping mulled wine and eating tasty sausages at the Rathaus Christmas markets in Vienna.

The first time we went to Berlin together, we landed at the famous Templehof Airport, where Hitler made lots of appearances. It also featured in le Carré and Len Deighton films, as I reminded Val at the time. I was pleased on that holiday that I could impress Val with my command of the German language and also with how to have a really grand German meal! Val wanted to go to an upmarket restaurant or hotel for our first night's dinner out but I would have none of it! I guided her to a nondescript *bier keller* down some grubby steps. She wasn't too happy when we entered the place, although it was very clean and spacious. Having found a comfortable table and settled down, I called a waitress and persuaded Val to let me order for both of us. The meal we had was 'out of this world', as I knew it would be, both in quantity and quality. Pork cutlets and *Wiener Schnitzel*, salad, fried potatoes and various sausages, followed by apple strudel and cream, several bottles of Rhine wine and a selection of bread and cheeses to follow. We could not eat it all; but Val did admit, after she had checked the bill, that it was good value and quite inexpensive. I did confess to Val afterwards that my RAF colleagues and I, many years before, had always used the beer cellars for our meals out. Good food, plenty of it and all reasonably priced.

The world is certainly getting smaller. I say this as I recall an incident that happened to us on one holiday in Austria. We were in our early seventies and enjoying a quieter holiday in the small resort of St Gilgen, not far from Salzburg. We were staying in a quite large apartment, self-catering, kindly rented to us by the parents of a friend of Val's, Louise. As we were older, we had visited Salzburg many times and had visited many of the tourist spots in the area. On this holiday, we had decided to act our age and take it easy for a change. Each day, after a leisurely breakfast in the apartment, we would set off on foot down a rather steep hill into the village centre; do a bit of shopping, sometimes have a coffee and decide what to do next. This often ended with a slow walk to the large lake, where many day-trippers would congregate. Val would usually have prepared an excellent packed lunch for us and we would find a convenient seat lakeside, where we would enjoy our lunch al fresco. There was always plenty to see by the lakeside in St Gilgen. We would watch the many tourist coaches disembark their excited visitors; these were mainly Japanese and rich Middle-Eastern people. They would all rush to get food and refreshments from the many cafés and stalls around the lake or join the queues for steamer trips on the large and attractive expanse of water surrounded by snow-capped mountains.

We were sitting there, having enjoyed our lunch, when I decided, with Val's permission, as she was a non-smoker all her life, to light up a pipe of St Bruno tobacco for my own selfish pleasure! Enjoying my smoke, I was suddenly aware of a smartly dressed middle-aged man and a lady, standing quite close to our seat. Wondering what they were up to, I turned and gave them a stare. I was then addressed by the man in German. He was very polite and apologetic in his manner, telling me that it was my St Bruno tobacco that had attracted him. He went on to say how wonderful and aromatic the distinct tobacco was. He praised it so much that I was really in quite a state of shock myself. Val could not understand what he was saying at first because it was in rapid German. After I had told him, in German, that we were holidaymakers from Exeter in England, he continued to speak in German but politely slowed down a little. He told me that he had attended Exeter University many years ago and that, as a fellow pipe-smoker, he had bought his St Bruno tobacco from McGahey's shop in Exeter's high street!

We continued to chat, as two couples, for some time, in German throughout, and he was delighted when I offered him a pipeful of St Bruno. The last we saw of him, he was strolling along the lakeside puffing away happily on his pipe, his wife in tow beside him! Having been a student at Exeter University myself, that two alumni should meet at the lakeside in St Gilgen, Austria, and have a common interest and a conversation about St Bruno tobacco and McGahey's shop in Exeter, is quite remarkable. It did provide Val and me with another fond memory over many years of many lovely holidays that we enjoyed in Austria. Val quickly became a fan of Austrian cuisine. She came to enjoy, as I did, the many pork dishes, *Weiner Schnitzel* in particular, the dumplings, strudel and other apple delights, Hungarian ghoulash soup and all the light lager beers!

Val and I both loved animals throughout our lives. Inevitably, on our travels, we would come across cruelty to animals and neglected animals in some countries. We were naturally upset about this and always made our views known to the local population, whenever possible.

That was never enough for Val, however. She was always determined to do something about it in a practical way. As a result, on many of our trips abroad, I would often be seen struggling to carry a holdall or bag laden with tins of Whiskas, Kattomeat and dog munchies. This was emergency food for any stray or feral cats, in particular, that we may come across on our holiday. I must admit that I have spent many nervous minutes just 'keeping an eye out', often feeling quite embarrassed, while Val fed stray cats in a foreign country. Locals would find it incredible that a well-dressed lady was feeding their wild population of felines. In fact, they would often openly laugh at us and ridicule us. In most countries, Val would buy cat food locally and I would be her assistant, opening tins and generally assisting in feeding an often ravenous group of half-wild cats of all shapes and sizes. We did this in Malta, Greece and France but most notably in Israel, including Jerusalem and the seaside town of Netanya. When I frequently brought up the subject with Val, her answer was always the same: at least the cats would be happy for once in their lives.

I should point out that we did not actively look for stray cats when we were on holiday. There were many occasions, however, when we could not avoid seeing some blatant examples of animal neglect and even cruelty. It is well known that donkeys are the subject of much abuse and ill treatment in many countries of the Middle East and in Greece. It is true today that in some countries things are changing. For example, in France and Malta, there are now organisations akin to our RSPCA who are beginning to address this ongoing problem of cruelty to animals. Val was particularly upset to witness the problem in Israel. Feeding stray cats in Israel, in Jerusalem, in fact, she once said to me, "How can this be tolerated here of all places? It's disgraceful, they should be ashamed." When I pointed out to her that many humans were being ill treated in Israel at that very time during conflicts, it did not help.

Chapter 9

Caring for Each Other

Val and I made some vows and promises to each other when we married on 26th October 1957.

"To live together after God's ordinance in the holy estate of matrimony – love her, comfort her, honour and keep her, in sickness and in health, and forsaking all others keep thee only unto her, so long as ye both shall live."

I said these words:

"I take thee Valerie to my wedded wife, to have and to hold from this day forward, for better for worse, for richer for poorer, in sickness and in health, to love and to cherish, till death do us part, according to God's holy ordinance, and thereto I plight thee my troth."

Val and I made promises to each other very early in our relationship. These vows were to remain with us throughout our sixty-one-year marriage. They were the foundation and guiding light of our journey together. That we were able to fulfil these promises is testimony to one thing: love. Our love was a gift from God; no one should doubt that. Now in the twilight years of my own life, I am convinced that our love affair and our happy marriage were gifts from God, a blessing.

We were both only happy when the other was happy. Conversely, we were unhappy when either of us was sad, anxious, in pain or worried in any way. Our love for one another meant that we always tried to care for each other. Ever-present was my desire to compensate for Val's poor start in life. I wanted to give her everything I could and do whatever I could to make her happy. There was also an overwhelming desire to thank her for caring for me so well over so many days and years. That is, of course, what love is all about. I think it helps if it is God-given and blessed by the Almighty. From those formal vows made in church in 1957, to Val's passing in 2019, we both did our best to keep our promises.

So, in this chapter, I will try to illustrate with examples and anecdotes our caring for each other and just how wonderful our long journey together has been. Hopefully, other couples who have been similarly blessed will understand and recognise much of what is written from their own experience. For example, it was not always necessary for me to say to Val "I love you." She knew it could be said simply with a look into her eyes; I knew that she knew!

Early in this story, mention was made of Val's disturbed and often unhappy childhood. The home she spent her early years in was not a pleasant one. It was certainly not one in which an only child could learn about love and kindness. Instead of developing as a child in a loving environment, she was in a frightening place full of lies, arguments and fights. Physical violence frequently occurred and she was subjected to this herself from a very young age. Over the years, Val was able to convey to me some detail and the horror of it all. This was something I found difficult to imagine myself, at the time. She felt very alone when she was little, closer to her mother, but bewildered and frightened most of the time. Recently, while I was sorting some things here in the bungalow, I came across an old diary of Val's. Some of the entries are relevant and illustrate her unhappiness and fears as a child.

She was writing in her diary to a cat that we had at the time. This was a rescued cat who had been badly treated, called 'Lavender'. She tells Lavender in the entry that she understands how she, the cat, feels:

'I know what it is like to be lonely and ill-treated just like you', she wrote. This was written in her thirties and I only came across it fifty years later! These experiences of her childhood never left her, and affected her throughout her future life.

Mention of our cat Lavender reminds me of another example of Val's caring nature. Our first cat, Fluffy, the one who cleared our cottage of mice some years before, had died on Boxing Day after more than fifteen years with us. We were upset and missed her dreadfully for several months afterwards. We were in our new house in Rowan Way, Exeter, and we agreed not to have another cat immediately as it inhibited our holiday travel plans. By then, I was a teacher, and we had already enjoyed many holidays together. We planned more holidays, so it made sense not to have pets at home for a while. Val and perhaps fate had other ideas!

Looking through the local paper one day, Val spotted an article about a cat and brought it to my attention. This article was headlined *'The Loneliest Cat in the World'* and it told of a small cat that had been ill-treated, which included burns and malnourishment. The accompanying photograph showed a thin, ugly little cat with no teeth. The article by the Cats Protection League went on to explain that lots of people had been to see the cat but all had turned her down. No one would take her. Val was devastated by the story. She pleaded with me that we could give her a home. I was adamant. We had agreed; no cats at this time. Val then started a campaign to change my mind! She kept on at me for more than a week. I found copies of the newspaper article in several parts of the house, in prominent places. Val would not give up. I finally gave in when I found a large photocopy of the article in the bathroom one morning when shaving and getting ready for work!

We went to see the cat that evening and when it leapt on Val's lap and began to purr, that was that, she became our second feline friend, already named Lavender due to her slightly coloured fur. I have a photograph of Val and Lavender together, which still brings a tear to my eye today.

I am convinced that Val found her faith in God during her teen years. She believed that God would give her a better life. As long as she believed and did her best to lead a good life, things would improve for her. When I met her, she was already living a good Christian life.

She went to church; she cared for others; she hated lies, swearing and violence and cruelty of any kind. She loved animals and did all she could to help the unfortunate. She was a lady in every sense and could not and would not stand bad language or dirty jokes at any time. She had excellent manners; she was modest and somewhat shy. She had already made great strides forward on her path to a good life when I met her. This continued during our courting days. She was so happy to be involved with a normal family life. On visits to my parents, and particularly to my elderly grandparents, Val always glowed with happiness. She would fuss around my folks, be attentive and helpful, and she patently enjoyed the loving family environment that she had not been used to herself. She quickly grew to love my grandparents in particular and often visited them when I was away in the RAF. This Val that I had fallen in love with showed equal care and love to me. She did so much for me from our early courting days and throughout our marriage. When we made those vows in 1957, we certainly meant them!

In her caring for me, I could not have asked for more throughout our marriage. She was always a little dynamo regarding work of any kind. She learned to cook from scratch and over the years she taught herself so well that she became an excellent cook. She would never admit this, of course! She frequently played down her skills and expertise. The fact is that I, many friends and family can testify to her prowess in the kitchen. Her cakes always sold quickly at various Cofton WI stalls in later years.

Her love for me shone through every day in our marriage. She nursed me through many illnesses, including bowel cancer in 1997. She worried about me when I was travelling anywhere; I remember vividly her concern if I was ever late home from school when on car journeys. She comforted me when I had a 'bad' day at work, and she always wanted to know what had happened during my work days. She would offer advice and support in everything I did, or wanted to do; she was my support and my everything! It could be summed up by simply saying that her life was dedicated to me in love, and I felt the same about her. She made it plain to me and others that she loved me deeply. Without doubt, her love for me was apparent in all our daily life together. She wanted me to be happy every day, and she did her best to see that this happened. She encouraged me to enjoy my hobbies; she would deliberately give me time and space. She knew I enjoyed watching sport, on TV and at games. In later years, I can 'see' her now, waving me off in my car going to watch a football game in Exeter with the words, "Enjoy the game, darling. I hope they win!"

On our delayed honeymoon in Edinburgh way back in 1958, Val readily and happily went with me to football matches. We saw Scotland play in an International at Hampden Park and Hibernian play at Easter Road Stadium, both during our belated honeymoon! Val was simply delighted that she had made me happy, although she didn't understand or like football at all!

These were not just isolated examples; she was always like this. The many memories that flood back to me now are so heart-warming. I could go on forever about the things that Val did for me. The washing, mending, ironing and the many homes she lovingly built for us.

The curtains she made, the gardening, painting and decorating that she was glad to do, at various homes. She had an artistic skill throughout her life; flower arranging, pictures and ornaments, her own excellent handwriting and her skill with words are testament, alongside her musical talent, to a very creative person. So much done, all happily, with love and pride in our life together.

In the first chapter, I tried to explain that when I met Val, I knew that this was different. She was special to me and I felt that 'spark' between us all those years ago back in 1955. She felt the same. One could say that it really was 'love at first sight'. To simply consider the facts offers ample evidence of this. I was used to having affairs and I had no intention of being serious in any of my relationships. I liked many of my girlfriends but I had never had the inclination to say "I love you" to any of them. Then I met Val and I knew this was different. Instead of just wanting to add her to my list of conquests, to try to seduce her, or play her along, I changed; it was quite amazing. Later, in our married life, I often told Val that 'Cupid's arrow' had landed in my heart on Christmas Eve 1955.

For Val, it was a similar story. After all, she was engaged to another young man when I met her! She had been through a proposal, met his family and had even started to get her trousseau together. She had accepted his proposal and she was wearing his engagement ring, on our very first date together. Within a few weeks, she had broken off her engagement and returned the ring. It is important to remember Val's circumstances at this time. She must have yearned to escape from her unhappy memories of her own parents and her own childhood nightmares. She faced opposition to any thought of her leaving her family home, where she was the only reason her parents were still together. She gave up the possibility of an early escape, for me! A significant personal decision to take.

It became clear to me in the early years of our marriage, and she told me many times, that she felt the 'spark' between us just as I had. She knew, just as I did, that our love was special, it was meant to be, a gift from the Almighty. Our love was a combination of both physical attraction and an emotional one. For the first time in our lives, we could look into each other's eyes, hold each other in a close embrace and say those magic words: *I love you*. More importantly, we both meant it sincerely and we couldn't help it! That such a natural attraction, a love and an understanding of each other could last for sixty-one years is quite remarkable to contemplate, a miracle. Of course, it has happened to other couples throughout history. To be blessed with it is wonderful and uplifting.

When thinking about a long and happy marriage, one inevitably asks the question of ourselves and of others, what's the secret ingredient? My immediate answer would have to be 'love'. We have all seen those interviews where this or a similar question is asked of couples on the occasion of their golden or even diamond wedding anniversaries. The answers given are usually along the lines of 'give and take' or 'compromise', or sometimes 'humour'. There are many others, of course.

When thinking about Val and me, inevitably one comes back to that magic word 'love'. However, one can break it down a little, to try to identify some of the factors which were patently important in maintaining a happy relationship for such a long time.

Val and I were different people and we came from very different backgrounds. Our childhood years were very different, mine certainly happier than Val's. Having said that, we did have lots in common; we both liked to travel, to explore new places. Alongside this was a love of history and a desire to learn from it. We both loved music and literature; our tastes were different but we were addicts to both throughout our life together. We both had an interest in, and were very fond of, animals; we had both been brought up to respect all animals, both pets and in the wild. This love for all fauna remained with us always, and our pets played an important part in our marriage. Importantly, we both had a moral base in Christianity and similar thoughts on our personal values; from Sunday school attendance, membership of the Girl Guides for Val and Boy Scouts for me, and an established sense of integrity. In Val's case, her faith was much stronger than mine. Her childhood experiences, in my view, shaped her belief in the Almighty early in her teens. When we married, she was already a very Christian lady who 'practised what she preached'.

We were both romantics, a very bold statement to make here! Val loved receiving a bouquet of flowers; she loved romantic novels; she loved music and poetry; she would be upset easily by cruelty of any kind; she wanted everyone to have a good life; she cared about the world and everyone in it. Although I sometimes maintained the appropriate macho-male image for obvious reasons, I secretly shared much of Val's romanticism. A practical example of this is the fact that I rarely, if ever, forgot our wedding anniversaries or Val's birthday. She received flowers and huge cards from me for most of our sixty-one-year marriage on each anniversary. She loved arranging flowers, and I was always delighted to watch her do it! Equally, I would love to give her many presents, keeping it secret until the last minute, then surprising her with something that she had secretly longed for; sometimes a plane ticket, a piece of jewellery, perfume or underwear. She once talked of getting herself some roller skates, so I bought her some! I bought her a surfboard and an expensive keyboard instrument, all of which were rarely used. It was worth it for me, just to see her face on the day! I too love poetry and we both shared a liking for reading biographies. I wonder what Val would think of this, my attempt at writing OUR own biographic-memoir.

Val was similarly romantic with me; throughout our marriage, she would buy me presents, often not for a special occasion, simply 'out of the blue'. Early in my teaching career, one of my schools got into music in a big way and all staff had to be involved. This was a disaster for me. Although I loved listening to music, both classical and popular, I was no musician! Val was, of course. While I was worrying myself sick about buying a triangle or something equally ridiculous, Val took action.

A few days later, I got home from school and she presented me with a second-hand guitar together with a manual, *Teach Yourself Simple Guitar*. She had travelled by train from Exeter to Newton Abbot to buy the guitar, having found and then responded to a private newspaper advert! Val then spent several weeks teaching me how to play simple chords and very simple tunes! The end result was that I received considerable praise for my very small contribution to the school's musical production; a few simple chords, I confess.

How could I not adore my lovely wife? This is but one small example of the mutual love and understanding, the caring and the deep love that we shared.

There were some things, understandably, that Val and I did not have in common. Our sense of humour was quite different. Val loved simple slapstick humour. She would curl up laughing at Laurel and Hardy, Morecambe and Wise or Ken Dodd. I was always way out in my comedy likes; The Goon Show, Terry Pratchett and others gave me great pleasure. We did over the years find some common ground regarding humour, however; the films of Mel Brooks being one such example. We both laughed at and enjoyed Brooks' comedies. Val particularly liked *The Producers*, *Stir Crazy* and *Blazing Saddles* as films, and we watched others, with Gene Wilder often in the cast.

This mutual liking we acquired of what is ostensibly Jewish humour must, to some extent, be linked to our common interest in Judaism and Israel. As I have touched on earlier, there was a Jewish line in my family, certainly on my maternal grandmother's side. Val could never explain how or why she was so interested in Judaism, particularly as she was a practising Christian. She was always fascinated with Judaism and the Jewish people and their history; this was, of course, reinforced on our five visits to Israel during our marriage. Our mutual love of history, literature and music must also have played a part. In hindsight, I also personally believe that Valerie identified with the great suffering that the Jewish people had endured over centuries; she was interested in the Holocaust, the World War 2 atrocities and Yad Vashem in Jerusalem. Our bungalow here today still contains many books relating to Israel, the Holocaust and personal biographies of Holocaust survivors, all read avidly by both of us, and somewhat treasured too.

I recall one day presenting Val with one particular book on Jewish life and humour: *'Funny.... You don't look Jewish',* by Sidney Brichto. She loved it and to be honest, so did I! I mention all this because it was something that Val and I always had in our marriage and it brought us much closer together. Perhaps it was another nudge from the Almighty. After all, it is the same Almighty for both Christians and Jews, in my view, although not in everyone's! We both loved to laugh at Jewish comedians like Jackie Mason. When in Israel, we both got along well with the locals of all religions. We had some interesting meetings and conversations there and we always felt good about that. It may seem strange that two Christians should feel so happy, contented and not one bit upset by such exposure to different faiths, but it was true. This fascination with Judaism brought Val and I even closer together over many years.

During the writing of this book and as a direct result of my daily recalling many memories of our life together, I realise how very much Val affected me and my development as an adult. Remembering her suffering as a child and the damage it did to her development as she grew up, reminds me every day of how that came to influence me. My constant awareness and a desire to ease her ever-present sadness and self-doubt enabled me to find the means to make her life a much happier one. Out of the tragic events of her early years came the promise of a solution. Things that I could do for her, words that I could say to her, love that I could demonstrate in a plausible, acceptable and practical way. My own life became dedicated to making her life better in any way that I could think of. It became my daily routine that I would do all in my power to please her. In practical terms, this meant me often giving way to her whims and fancies, and I would sometimes give in to something that my very being disliked or even hated. This was clearly illustrated in our various homes over the years. Furnishings, ornaments and even light fittings were all of Val's choice. When tempted to say, *I don't like that, I'd prefer this*, I didn't speak up, deliberately. When her face lit up and she was obviously happy with something, I would endorse her views, agree with her and let her have her own way. Now, all these years on, I'm glad that I did it; gave in to her, made that little moment pleasant for her, gave her something, however small, that made her happy. I knew that I couldn't change what had happened in those early years, but in a tiny way I could improve her life. A considerable part of this was my desire to enable her to travel. As a young girl, largely through reading and dreaming about the things and places she read about, she always longed to travel extensively. I was able to fulfil those dreams for her and it made her very happy over more than fifty years. Because I loved her so, that made me happy too.

I am writing this during Advent 2020 with the Christmas festival fast approaching. It is a time when we remember dear friends and loved ones, still with us and some who have 'passed over Jordan', as my grandmother used to say. It has naturally sharpened many thoughts and emotions in me. This is my second Christmas without Val here beside me. It has already brought back vivid memories of the two of us preparing for Christmas.

I remember so clearly with much love and happiness the little things we did together. Preparing the bungalow, putting up all the cards and particularly decorating the Christmas tree. Val was good at it. She had a natural artistic flair and I would always follow her instructions. As a result, we had it all. Various candles, tree, festive tablecloth and napkins; the silver candelabra would come out of hiding, be polished and furnished with new candles. It was all quite magical for weeks before Christmas, and we both loved it. I always felt a warm glow just seeing Val so happy. She would work so hard at it; she would write some eighty or so Christmas cards, many with letters enclosed, and they would go across the globe. She would make endless trips to the shops; small Christmas items that she had lovingly bought years ago on trips to the Christmas markets in Vienna were carefully extracted from their hiding places to go on show. We would always try to surprise each other with regard to presents. Several would be exchanged on Christmas morning and Val would always keep a surprise package which she would pretend to have forgotten and give to me in the afternoon. She loved doing this and I often did the same to her. I remember with much joy now our Christmas evenings together. A glass or two of wine and a magnificent supper, lovingly prepared by Val, with her home-cooked ham, a splendid variety of cheeses, pickles, and so on, this followed by a whisky for me and Val's favourite tipple, Courvoisier brandy and a little dry ginger.

We have all heard it said that one can die of a broken heart. There have been many recorded cases of the death of a husband or wife not long after their loved one's demise, so it does happen. Of course, the death certificate issued does not record the death as 'broken heart'; however, I do now believe much more that such things are possible. Where do these thoughts come from in me? I have over the last few days found myself increasingly simply sitting in a comfortable armchair and thinking. My thoughts are always about Val and I and our life as a married couple for some fifty-eight years, that is, excluding our last three years together after the onset of Val's stroke and illness.

My thoughts cover many years, at random. I am in awe of them all. From the two of us chasing each other on a beach when we were young, and collapsing in giggles into an embrace, to my awakening from a life-threatening major cancer operation in hospital in Exeter and seeing Val's face smiling down on me. It has all been a wonderful journey, but the here and now is simply sadness that she is no longer here with me. We had a remarkable marriage. I worshipped the ground that she walked upon and there is no doubt that she idolised me and loved me deeply. She was always there for me; she could put things right; she seemed to know my thoughts almost before they had formed in my head. We had a mutual understanding and love that was magical between us. We instinctively knew if one of us was worried or unhappy in the slightest way and we could do something about it. Sometimes that involved a close embrace and kisses, but frequently it was simply resolved by a look, a few words, and just holding hands for a while. The amazing thing about such love is this understanding and togetherness still happened even if we were far apart. I can recall many times when I telephoned Val from afar and we found we had been thinking the same thoughts and had often already reached the same conclusion. We were as one for more than fifty years in a variety of situations, places and times. That being so, it is little wonder that I now feel at this time that I am 'broken-hearted' to have lost my Valerie, that an emptiness creeps over me, great sadness and loneliness. Luckily, I am able to fight these feelings of despair and be successful. I make myself concentrate on a particular time in our life together, remember as many tiny details as possible and force myself to conjure up scenes which we played out in some bygone year. It is not always easy to do, but it has sustained me these recent days.

Writing this book, I have had to recall so many memories. This has had a profound effect on me as a person. Although I always tried to live a decent life with integrity and Christian values at its core, I know I have failed at times. Val's love and her wonderful caring nature have made me reflect on my own values, and I know that I can do better. It is patently obvious to me now that she was so good for me. Over many years, her influence gave me the desire and the strength to contribute something to others. In my teaching career, in particular, Val's support was significant. Now I often find myself thinking, *what would Val have done or advised me to do?* Our love lives on in this way, beyond the grave. It is another lasting testament to our love and marriage that I now have a strong faith in the Almighty; Val had this throughout her time on Earth. I tried at all times to make Val happy and to compensate her for her unhappy childhood. She gave me so much back that it changed my life for the better, and I will be eternally grateful for that.

Early in 1997, at the age of sixty-one, I was diagnosed with bowel cancer. This resulted in major surgery followed by twenty weeks of chemotherapy and some radiotherapy. Luckily, I got through it all and survived. This was in no small measure due to the post-operative care I received from my dear wife, Val. She was magnificent throughout. She was under enormous stress in the week after my operation and in the following weeks, when I was having to go to the hospital on a weekly basis for the chemo, worrying that things would not go well and having to cope with the considerable side effects of the chemo which I was suffering. She knew she might lose me. In the early weeks of my recovery, she fielded all the daily calls from my work colleagues, family and friends. She remained remarkably calm and handled everything with cheerful optimism. She continued to shower me with all the love that she could give me, day and night.

She often told me that our well-loved and rather old cat, Gizmo, did suffer too on occasion.

While I was in the hospital, Val would visit me daily. She insisted on making her own way from Dawlish to the Royal Devon and Exeter Hospital by bus. She declined kind offers of lifts, she said, in order to give herself 'thinking time'. When she returned from the visit, she would make a fuss of the cat while often eating a warmed-up stew she had made, with Gizmo on her lap. She told me how the cat would get annoyed each evening because no sooner had she sat down with the cat and her stew, than the telephone would ring. She would leap up, casting the cat and her stew aside and rush to the phone. I believe that the cat got so used to this performance that she would leap off Val's lap as soon as the phone rang!

After some months of recovery, I eventually went back to teaching, on a part-time basis. Val had fresh worries then because I was driving myself to Somerset three days each week. She was so relieved each evening when my car arrived in our driveway, and she always greeted me with a hug and a kiss. Later that year, we decided to try to have a holiday in the UK. We took the train to Edinburgh and spent ten days or so there. During the first post-op holiday, we were very pleased to meet up with an ex-teaching colleague of mine, and a friend to both of us, who was then teaching in Edinburgh. We had previously entertained the couple and their children in Exeter years before and we kept in touch. The first holiday, therefore, after my cancer became quite a milestone and an enjoyable break for both of us. It was lovely for me to see Val relax and enjoy herself again.

To see her laughing after the year we had endured, socialising normally again, lifted my spirits considerably.

In subsequent years after the 'cancer year' of 1997, we got back to our annual holidays and travel. Scotland and Cornwall came back on our list and we decided to try to go further afield. There were a few hurdles to overcome, however, for me. One difficulty was the state of what was left of my alimentary canal. Since the operation, I had to be careful what I ate and when I ate it. Val was always a superb cook and she knew exactly what I could or could not eat safely. She had taken all the medical and dietary advice on board, and as a result, I rarely had any trouble when eating at home. On holiday, particularly on the Continent, I regularly had problems, however. Suffice to say that over the following few years I became very familiar with the public toilet facilities in Rome, Prague, Antibes, Vienna and some quite remote villages in Austria!

When I had to find toilet facilities in a hurry, Val was always very supportive and her loving self. She would check out the available public loos in whatever country or city we were in, keeping me informed at all times when we were sightseeing. Nevertheless, things did go wrong sometimes. On one notable occasion in France, we were staying in an apartment in Antibes and on a day visit to Cannes, when my tummy decided to play up. I desperately ran along the prestigious Croisette in Cannes by the Film Festival theatre looking for the public toilets that Val had assured me were there. They were there all right, but closed for a lunch break! Panic quickly set in for me, but Val, ever calm and resourceful, pointed to the posh restaurant facing the theatre.

We ran across the square and staggered into a very upmarket restaurant. Val took charge and using her excellent French, with an accent that would put Bardot to shame, told the very attentive waiter that we would be dining at the window table, but first that *Monsieur*, meaning me, wished to inspect the toilet facilities. I was extremely relieved to make it to a magnificent, gold-plated toilet suite, worthy of film stars, complete with a revolving toilet seat and all the necessary accoutrements. Some twenty minutes later, I rejoined Val at her table, where she was sipping a glass of wine. We both often remembered that day in Cannes, I for obvious reasons, Val disappointed that she didn't get to see Clint Eastwood, who was on a yacht in the Cannes marina at the time!

Another occasion comes to mind when my need for an emergency visit to public toilets caused a problem, this time for Val. We were staying in Prague at the time and Val wanted to visit the Jewish area to look around the famous Jewish cemetery there. As mentioned elsewhere, although a devout Christian herself, Val had always taken great interest in Israel and Jewish life. We had already visited Israel on five separate holidays by the year 2000. So on this day in Prague we set off with our street map to find the Jewish Quarter. Eventually, by mid-afternoon, we found it; we had already had our lunch. I suddenly gave Val the 'danger' signal, meaning that I would urgently require toilets. Luckily, we did not have to look far. There, just a few metres from the entrance to the Jewish cemetery and museum, we spotted a large underground toilet facility. Eagerly clutching my shoulder bag containing my medical needs, I vanished down the steps and into the gents'. Unfortunately, what was left of my large and small colons decided to play trick after trick on me at once. As a result, it was some half-hour before I emerged up the steps from the toilet. I could not see Val anywhere! In a state of some panic I rushed about and finally caught sight of her in a doorway around the corner. It appeared to me that a rather large man seemed to be bothering her, so I ran up to them, quite angry and in a rather threatening manner. Val told me to calm down, saying over and over again, "It's okay, John, it's all okay." It transpired that while Val was waiting for me, for half an hour, she had been loitering with possible intent, and this large raincoated man was a special undercover policeman of sorts, guarding the Jewish Quarter and the nearby Jewish Museum. He wanted to know what she was up to! She was a lady in her late sixties then and what on earth they thought she was up to, I'll never know. We did laugh about it back at our hotel but it was quite a shock at the time. Val joked that she must look like Mata Hari or a terrorist. The policeman had shown us his identity card and had apologised profusely after I had joined Val. It seems that after our adventures with the Mossad in Israel, we were not free from the attentions of security services on our travels, even in the Czech Republic! It gave us something else to remember Prague for, apart from the Vltava River and the Charles Bridge. Val's favourite composer was the Czech Smetana, and his symphony *Má Vlast* (*My Fatherland*) was played at her funeral.

On another holiday, Val enjoyed a boat trip along the Vltava River which runs through Prague. She became the star among many nationalities of visitors on board that day; she was able to take over from a delighted young male tour guide with a short biography of Bedrich Smetana, the Czech composer, and an explanation of the movements of his most famous work *Má Vlast*, which was being played as we sailed up the river. We were rewarded later with free afternoon tea and cakes on the boat!

Although it may be hard to believe, Val and I had very few arguments or rows during our many years together. I cannot honestly remember one really bad time between us. Not once in sixty-one years of marriage did either of us threaten to leave the other or actually walk out. I am aware that I gave in to her too easily if we disagreed about something. I had this thing that was always in the back of my mind about her childhood being so sad and unhappy for her. I suppose I was obsessed really with keeping her happy. As a result, I often went against my better judgement and simply 'caved in'. It was often over quite trivial things, like a choice of furnishings or even a meal. Sometimes they were, of course, important things, such as moving house to Dawlish to live in 1996. Val wanted us in our retirement years to live beside the sea. She chose Dawlish and she also chose the bungalow that I still live in today. It is true that I was also reasonably happy with these choices at the time. It is, however, significant that I have already changed some of the external features and internal fittings and furniture since Val's death.

Going back to consideration of our arguments or disagreements, we wouldn't ever let them continue to fester in any way, whenever they occurred. We never went to bed 'not talking' to each other. We made a rule for ourselves in our first year of marriage that if we were unhappy or angry about anything it had to be resolved before we went to bed. It worked for us. We always had a special kiss in bed last thing to prove it and we would say those three little words, I love you. We didn't ever go in for long silences or not talking to one another. I was lucky because Val was very ticklish. If she ever seemed to me to be down or a little grumpy, I would simply tickle her somehow and she was soon laughing and urging me to stop. This would be followed by a kiss and a cuddle. If I was likewise grumpy or down for some reason, Val would spot it quickly and use her considerable feminine charms on me. That always worked!

One of the main reasons that we rarely had rows or words was because of the respect and love we had for one another, but there were also other reasons. From early in our marriage, we gave each other space. We both had different friends, often long-standing and trusted friends. We didn't interfere in those relationships; we tolerated each other's friends and allowed these friendships to continue and flourish. Maybe I should hasten to add that these were same-gender friends, women for Val, chaps for me.

We also both had different interests and hobbies and we allowed time for that without impinging on one another's interests. Having said that, we did also share many things, like literature and music. Unlike some couples, we were quite happy to be pursuing different interests at the same time, in the same house. This would often be me indulging in my amateur radio hobby with headphones on, while Val was either reading or playing the piano.

We did, of course, also do a lot together, and we managed to create situations where we combined the two, and this created a form of harmony rather than conflict. We were always happy in each other's company and always shared our thoughts. That was important for both of us; we could talk to each other always and, over the years, we even developed a sort of sixth sense when there was a problem or a difficulty. We didn't keep secrets from one another. Like most happily married couples, we were honest and open in discussing both pleasant and unpleasant things. We would resolve the problems with large doses of compromise. Also, like most happily married couples, we enjoyed the fact that we could resolve minor disagreements quickly and without anger or bitterness. The loving and often amorous aftermath on such occasions were rewarding for both of us. They are remembered with great pleasure, even now!

Bringing all this back to mind encourages more thoughts of Val's loving and caring nature; not just for me but for many others throughout her life. The fact that she had so many dear friends, that these friendships flourished and lasted for so long and that they were valued so much, is testimony to the caring and loving person that she was. Since her passing, I have received many letters and personal comments about how Val affected many others' lives in a significant way. It is heartwarming and quite wonderful to discover some of these things, although I was already aware of many of them.

Her diaries, which she kept meticulously for many years, reveal a lot about her friendships. I have to admit here that I have not, and will not, read all of her diaries. They were her private thoughts and I do not feel entitled to pry into them. Our marriage was so strong, our love so deep, that she told me, during our life together, most of what is written in her diaries.

I have read a few entries, however; this is often as a result of accidental occurrences, pages torn and found in strange places, and so on. One or two of these have been mentioned in the pages of this book.

I have been a football fan most of my life. My interest in football started when I was at primary school; from kicking a ball about in the playground during the late forties through various local football teams as a teenager to watching my local football team, Exeter City, as a fan. Although I enjoyed it immensely, I soon realised that although I was physically well fitted to play the game, I was not a naturally gifted footballer. I knew what to do but sadly my physical skills couldn't match my brain in application. I accepted that I was not going to be a Stanley Matthews or Bobby Charlton. That did not dampen my interest in football, however. I became a typical fan, following the national team, the First Division clubs, as it was in those days, and my local team. When at the age of eleven I passed my eleven-plus and moved to the local grammar school, soccer was out. Grammar schools only played rugby!

The same thing happened; although I was fit enough and had the required physique, rugby union was enjoyable but not really my forte. In those days, one had no choice. As a result, I would spend my weeks playing rugby on Wednesdays and watching Exeter City play football on a Saturday. My father was an avid football fan and he took me to watch Exeter City play in 1947, standing on the terraces at St James' Park.

This addiction to football continued throughout my life and is still with me today. Val, my dear wife, accepted it and, although not a fan herself, she understood what it meant to me. She always encouraged me to watch matches and in our later years, she would cheerfully wave me off as I drove to Exeter or Torquay for a football match. I mentioned elsewhere that she happily joined me at big matches when on our delayed honeymoon in Scotland. She was pleased to see me enjoying myself and happy; she loved me. I did always make sure that she had a hot drink and a pasty at half-time when she was with me; she liked that!

This reminds me of another classic example of Val's caring nature and her love for me. We were settled in our bungalow here in Dawlish in the 2000s. I had retired from teaching, recovered from cancer and life was good for both of us. We were still having several holidays each year, usually two in the UK plus regular trips to Cornwall, and at least one Continental holiday. Part of this good life for me was continuing trips to watch Exeter City home games every other Saturday. Like most fans at that time, I stood on the terraces with the same group of 'football friends'. We would have refreshments together and occasionally meet before a game, and so on. Over the years, Val got to know some of my football friends and even met some before a match in Exeter. She would sometimes accompany me in the car to Exeter, where I would go to the football and she would either do some shopping or visit her friends in the city. I would make sure that she had a key to the car and she would be sitting in it patiently waiting for me to join her after the match.

It was October and as my birthday on the 21st approached, Val told me that she would take me out to lunch on the day at one of our local hotels, the Langstone Cliff, as a treat. I was happy with that. She told me that she had booked a table. On arrival at the hotel, we had pre-lunch drinks in the bar. I was suddenly surprised with a 'Happy Birthday' from a couple who entered the bar. It was my football friend, Alex Reid, a Scot, and his wife, Margaret. Having found their telephone number somehow, Val had invited them to join us for my birthday lunch as a surprise for me. What a wife, lover and caring person! It had taken her a lot of effort just to give me a lovely and very pleasant day. We all had an excellent meal and lots of laughs that day, recounting football and travel stories. We naturally talked a lot about our many trips to Scotland and my Scottish connections. My father was brought up in Perth; Alex was a Scot and they had spent a lot of time there. Alex met Margaret in the South West when he was serving with the Royal Marines in the West Country.

As a follow-up to Val's birthday surprise for me, I reciprocated at her next birthday on the following 21st of January. I am pleased to say that in the following three months or so, Val had no idea that I was plotting a similar surprise for her. I gave considerable thought to whom I would invite as a pleasant surprise for her. Some of her dearest friends lived a long way from Dawlish, so that posed problems in making secret arrangements. Her birthday fell mid-week, so that added to my problems. Also, some of the possible invitees were not well, fighting illnesses or facing operations; it was a difficult decision to make. The main criteria for me in deciding was that it had to be someone who would make Val happy instantly by their sudden unexpected appearance. I got on the telephone and began making arrangements, secretly. I invited Bob Wilson and his wife, Dee. He was a former professional footballer, had been our neighbour in Rowan Way in Exeter years ago. Readers will know him from an earlier chapter in this book. We had been friends for more than forty years and always kept in touch by telephone, letters and cards. I felt sure that Val, who was quite fond of Bob, would be delighted. Bob and Dee kept up the subterfuge and I booked a table for four at the Langstone Cliff Hotel. It was with some difficulty that I managed with various ploys to keep it from Val. I still did what I had always done as her birthday approached. I bought her presents, a large card and ordered flowers to be delivered on the day. Val went through the usual things as the day approached.

"What shall I wear?" The usual question, which I remember answering in my own usual way. She had her visit to the hairdresser the day before her birthday as usual. On the day, I was more nervous than Val. I gave her my presents, card and lots of hugs and kisses. The huge bouquet of flowers arrived later in the morning to Val's usual comment of "You shouldn't have spent so much on me."

She was, however, delighted with all the fuss I was making; she couldn't hide her feelings. To see my wife so happy, arranging the flowers in vases and getting ready for our meal out, gave me a warm inner glow; it always did!

We arrived at the Langstone Cliff Hotel on time and we were shown to a table. It was, of course, laid up as a table for four! Val was quick to spot this and started to look just a little nervous. I wouldn't answer her questions secretly, hoping that our guests would not be late. I was right. Bob and Dee arrived, dressed immaculately, with Dee holding a large bouquet of flowers and a card for Val. I watched as Val stood up to greet them with a large smile on her face, embraced our two guests and was obviously delighted with my choice!

It was a lovely occasion and a lovely surprise for Val; she had always had a soft spot for Bob, I knew that. He was a handsome, fit man and he was equally fond of Val. To see my darling wife so pleasantly surprised, glowing with so much happiness and talking excitedly with Bob and Dee was wonderful to behold. I felt good too. I know that this was what true love was all about.

'The day went well', to use the old cliché, and it remains clearly in my bank of lovely memories.

Chapter 10

In the Bedroom

In the first few years of our marriage, Val would often have some searching questions for me. These would come out of the blue. Usually, when we were in bed. Often, after we had been making love. She would pull me close to her and cuddle up to me. I would protest that I was exhausted, thinking that she wanted to restart our lovemaking! She would deliberately tease me, caress me and make exaggerated love to me. Then she would pose the questions.

"How come you are so good at sex?" This would continue for some time.

"You must have had a lot of experience and lots of lovers."

Somehow, I managed to say that it was born in me and try not to answer any of these questions; often with great difficulty! After a while, thankfully, she would give up and we would fall asleep in each other's arms.

She was right, of course; she had guessed correctly. I was sexually active from my early teens. My testosterone levels had always been high and my interest in the opposite sex started at an early age. I had been intimate with several different women before Val. Some of these had been older than me and very experienced. They had been excellent teachers for me and I was secretly delighted with my early experiences of sex. Val knew this, she sensed it early in our marriage and I know that she didn't ever believe me when I told her it was innate and I was simply born lucky to have such skills!

That I had this early life experience and very good teachers in my early lovers was a blessing. It was something that I brought to our marriage and which helped us to make our early years together quite wonderful.

In sixty-one years of marriage, I never told Val anything about my pre-marriage affairs. She managed to discover some of the names of my previous girlfriends but that was all. She did make some quite accurate guesses on some occasions, but I always changed the subject adroitly. The facts were simply that I was quite experienced and proficient in bed with Val and that she was inexperienced, naïve and innocent, when we married. I was certainly to be her teacher in sexual matters and she was the student in 1957. Many years later, our roles were to be somewhat reversed. The student became more expert than the teacher. If you can imagine such a scenario, it was the making of an ideal physical relationship that was to remain with us for more than fifty years.

I must confess that this chapter is the most difficult one to write for obvious reasons. Writing a work of fiction, a romantic novel or a book aimed at a particular audience, a racy erotic novel, perhaps, I would find comparatively easy. I would let my imagination run riot and see what it produced. I am not doing that, however. I am writing a true story, a biographic memoir of my sixty-one years of marriage to my darling wife, Valerie. To write anything about the intimate and very private part of our marriage is difficult and certainly challenging. So why do it? I am doing it because I am convinced that it is necessary if I am to convey to the reader the full depth of our love for each other. The physical side of any marriage is important, as is the emotional side; it is without doubt an integral part of it. It cannot simply be ignored. It would leave a gap in a true love story that cannot be justified.

I have mentioned Val's modesty elsewhere; she was quite old-fashioned in many ways, not a prude, but a real lady. She was always careful in her choice of clothes. She would not reveal too much of herself in public. Therefore, one would never see Val in an off-the-shoulder dress, no bra straps would be seen, no cleavage revealed or any glimpse of thigh from a short skirt. I remember buying her a bikini swimsuit when we were in the prime of our life, our thirties. She tried it on and I was allowed to see her in it in our bedroom. She looked gorgeous and I told her so. She had a lovely body; she was slim, shapely, just over five foot, a seven-stone lovely lady in her prime. We had been happily married for years at the time but her response to my joy and delight, my visible excitement and my praise at her appearance was to blush and insist that it wasn't her. She wore the bikini only once in public on a beach, and then she spent the day draped in a rather large beach towel! That was my darling Val.

My point here is to emphasise that she was modest possibly to a fault sometimes in public, but she was so different, thank goodness, in private when alone with me. She was a wonderfully uninhibited, almost wanton and brazen, lover in her private life with me. She was innovative, inventive and lively in the bedroom; there is little doubt in my mind that I have never, and will never, come across another woman who is a better exponent of sexual acts. This woman, who would be embarrassed to show an inch of cleavage in public, became a skilled, desirable and quite expert lover in private.

During our courting days, our sexual activity was very limited. As already mentioned in earlier pages, this was confined to kisses, close embraces and not much more. There were two reasons for this. Firstly, Val's natural modesty and innocence; secondly, my reluctance to upset her or hurt her feelings in any way whatsoever. With my previous girlfriends, it was certainly different. Heavy petting was the norm after a couple of dates. Valerie was my first real love and I knew it. We did naturally get excited when in a close embrace on dates and on the way home from dates. There were times when I could have easily taken advantage of the situation but I deliberately refrained. It all changed a few weeks before our wedding in 1957 on that fateful trip to the chalet Seaview in Dawlish Warren. I will not repeat here what has been written in an earlier chapter about that momentous day. Our Wedding Night in Taunton has already been mentioned.

The physical side of our marriage did get off to a really perfect start. I was gentle, careful, caring and very slow and methodical in making love to Val. From the start I knew that a tender, deliberately careful approach was necessary. Val liked the soft, loving caress, not for her the rough ultra-macho action; I cannot remember ever throwing her down on a bed in passion in sixty-one years. It is quite understandable that Val wanted a gentle, sensitive lover after a childhood of experiencing violence to herself and what she had seen in her home. As a result, our lovemaking in the first few years of our marriage was superb. Foreplay by me initially always dominated any lovemaking. It soon became an art for both of us, in time; I was quite good at it from my previous experience and this was a great help. Suffice to say that Val loved it; her physical response from the start was remarkable. She always had orgasms and she was a fast learner. Her modesty outside the bedroom was still there, but in the bedroom, our lovemaking blossomed on a daily basis.

She gave herself wholeheartedly to me, with an increasing intensity as the months went by. I could not have experienced a more satisfying start to the intimate side of our marriage, and it was the same for Val.

She often spoke of our active sex life throughout the years. She was amazed to discover after conversations with her female friends that many women did not have happy sexual experiences. She told me that some had told her that orgasms were infrequent or even unknown. Her friends could not believe that Val was so happy with the physical side of her marriage. Val found this astonishing.

The real reason why the physical side of our marriage was so good is not hard to discover. It can be explained quite simply in one word: love. We loved each other very much and making love embodied that love, nurtured it and gave real expression to it. I was always gentle, loving and trying to give her what I thought she wanted. I was always quickly aware of her physical needs if there was a sudden change. We both wanted to please and satisfy each other in bed and we did. Throughout our many years together, I never once forced my attentions on Val; there were naturally times when I wanted to make love to her from a purely physical point of view and I knew that it wasn't an appropriate time for her or she was unresponsive for some other reason. As the years went by, we instinctively knew when it was going to happen. We both sensed it in a quite remarkable way. It may have been a look in each other's eyes, a gentle squeeze of a hand or even sometimes a blatant overt look or word. We both knew when we wanted to make love together, be it on getting ready for bed, in bed, or more frequently in our younger days, at any time during the day. It wasn't always in bed or even in the bedroom. We were always glad that we had carpeted floors in our homes, and lots of cushions!

During the fifty-eight years that Val and I slept together, neither of us ever used the proverbial excuse, "Sorry, I have a headache." As I have said already, I never once forced my attentions on her and she didn't ever have to do that to me. I was never rough with her either; she didn't like that for obvious reasons. Nevertheless, we had a very full and adventurous love life. We experimented and Valerie the student became Valerie the mistress in bed. What is truly rather special too is that our lovemaking continued into old age. Although it is true that the frequency naturally dropped, the success and the pleasurable orgasms for both of us stayed with us into our late seventies.

There are a few things that I should mention which are certainly appropriate for this chapter and no other. One is regarding the fact that this active sex life that we both enjoyed over fifty-eight years did not produce any children. Secondly, the wonderful way that it contributed to the strength of our marriage in the fact that neither of us were unfaithful or had any desire to be so or to break our marriage vow, 'Keep ye only unto her/him'. Thirdly, the way that our sex life was affected by my being struck down with cancer in 1997 at the age of sixty-one.

In the early years of our marriage, like most couples, we practised some form of contraception. The exception being, as the reader will already know, that day at the chalet before we married. In our late twenties, we did try for children without success. We even attended the RD&E Hospital on several occasions, going through all the necessary tests regarding fertility. In those days, there were no IVF clinics or other avenues to pursue. We were told eventually that there was no reason why Val shouldn't conceive. In other words, they said we should keep trying and it was up to the Almighty or fate. It simply did not happen for us. Many years later, several doctors, including psychiatrists, have hinted to me that the cause was probably linked to Val's childhood and her early experiences in life. In other words, it was the emotional scars or a mental block which resulted in her infertility. We were never to know. One thing that did change regarding the physical side of our marriage was that from the age of thirty-one, we no longer used any form of contraception. In a way, that quite naturally enhanced still further an already quite marvellous active sex life for us, if that was possible.

An anecdote is worth recording here. When Val was in the last months of her life at the Glenkealey Care Home in Teignmouth, she would often get up in the night and find her way to the home's kitchen in search of a sandwich or a cup of tea. The staff were very kind and indulged her whims. She would spend time talking to the night care staff. A senior carer, Rachel, told me that on one occasion she had been talking to Val in the middle of the night in the kitchen. She asked Val why we did not have any children, as we were such a happily married couple and had been together for so long. Evidently, Val became quite indignant in her reply. "It wasn't for want of trying, you know!" Although at the time dementia was beginning to take its toll on Val's thinking, she was clearly referring to our sex life together, and she wanted Rachel to know that it had been good and very active.

It is really a quite astonishing fact that over our sixty-one-year marriage, neither of us broke that sacred marriage vow of being faithful one to the other. Another anecdote at the end of this chapter may illustrate this. The fact that we never even considered looking elsewhere for romance or sexual liaisons of any sort is testament to our deep love. On the physical side, my needs did not lessen or wane over the years, but they were always adequately met with Val; I had no need or desire to seek excitement or diversions elsewhere. Over the years, Val developed and honed her mastery of lovemaking in all its forms. Similarly she was always happy and fulfilled in the physical side of our marriage. It was always quite obvious to me, but she also insisted on telling me throughout the years.

Of course, throughout our long marriage, we both had opportunities to stray should we have wanted to do so. There were a few occasions when I became jealous of the attentions of another man towards Val; at parties or dances when we were younger. Perhaps Val's dancing partner who got too close to her while dancing, or an overattentive young man. I knew that I could trust Val, but my male ego always made me intervene in some way to let the chap know that she was mine, so hands off! Similarly Val would quickly let any female predator, as she would call them, know that I was not available. We would usually end up having a laugh about it later on in the night, often in bed. In our younger years, it was more difficult for Val because I was often away from her due to my work. That's when I could say that I not only had the opportunities to stray but also faced the temptation. She knew such scenarios were bound to occur. She often talked of the times when I must have been tempted in our younger years, particularly when I was a teacher. She would discreetly mention a particular divorcee or single teacher who also happened to be an attractive woman. I always did my best to reassure her, and I must have made hundreds of telephone calls to Val when we were apart simply to try to put her mind at rest or tell her that I loved her. There was never any question of me succumbing to another woman's charms and Val knew it. I never looked at another woman in that way throughout our marriage and now, after all these years, I feel so happy that I was able to resist some of those temptations and remain faithful to the love of my life.

Early in 1997, I was diagnosed with cancer. We were devastated. At the age of sixty-one, I was still working full time as a teacher and Head of Department in a secondary school. Although I had been aware of possible medical problems in the previous year, I hadn't acted on the signs. Luckily, I didn't wait too long and took action in January 1997. I clearly remember the consultant telling me that he wouldn't know how long I had left to live until he had 'opened me up'. This was in response to my demand for an honest opinion on my life chances. It was colon cancer and I knew that the survival chances were better if caught early. In the few days we had before my urgent surgery, Val and I literally clung to each other. I took myself off in the bungalow and wrote several A4 pages to Val, put them in a large envelope and sealed it. I opened my heart to her in those pages and thanked her for the wonderful forty years of marriage we had experienced and for all that she had done for me. The envelope was addressed to Val and annotated with instructions *'only to be opened on my death'*. I still have that envelope with its contents today. It is still unopened. One day, I will open it and reread what I wrote to Val, twenty-five years ago, when I thought that I might die.

After major surgery, radiotherapy and twenty weeks of chemotherapy, I was cleared of the cancer and still alive! This quite naturally took its toll on our sex life. The chemotherapy was the hardest to endure with all its terrible debilitating side effects. The surgery also affected my sexual performance, with damage to the nervous system in the lower part of my body.

I am going to indulge myself here with an anecdote from this period when I was undergoing chemotherapy on a weekly basis. My oncologist at the RD&E Hospital, Dr Tony Nethersall, thought it would be helpful if I had a Hickman line put in my chest to facilitate easier application of the chemo. I agreed and he fitted the tube into my chest and I walked out of the hospital with a tube strapped across my chest. This worked well for my first few weekly visits to the oncology department. During the first six weeks after my surgery in 1997, after returning home, our sex life consisted of hugs, kisses and long embraces only. This was natural; Val treated me with the utmost care and love, like a delicate flower! However, we both felt the need to restart things in bed. I wanted to know that I could still perform, and Val simply loved me and she missed our active sex life. As a result, we did become more active in bed while I was still receiving weekly chemotherapy. I was relieved and Val was very happy with her first orgasm in many weeks and we fell asleep in each other's arms.

The following morning, I awoke with a dreadful pain in my left arm, which had also become badly swollen. Our overexuberant sexual activity had resulted in movement of the Hickman line tube inside my chest, which produced a thrombosis or blood clot in my arm. I was that day rushed to the RD&E Hospital, where I spent a week being treated for the thrombosis, successfully, thank goodness. I never let on to my cancer surgeon, oncologist or the many consultants and radiologists who treated me through this emergency that our lovemaking the night before was the cause! That they guessed correctly at the cause is beyond reasonable doubt.

Needless to say, Val and I resorted to more gentle hugs and kisses for a few weeks after that; to think that our love and our need for restarting our active sex life almost cost me my life when I had just escaped death from colon cancer. I am now even more convinced that the Almighty had a hand in my survival at this time; I was to have twenty-two more years of life with my beloved wife, Val.

Those bonus years were to see a change in our physical relationship, in our sex life. The damage to my body was significant; it did not affect my sex drive or libido in any way, but it did change my performance. We were aware of this and we modified things considerably in bed. However, I can honestly say throughout those last twenty years together we adapted well and that we were both able to satisfy our physical needs in bed. Before she died, Val often told me how she was amazed that we still managed the physical side of our love life and how wonderful it had been. I distinctly remember her turning to me in bed, after our lovemaking, hugging me and saying "that was lovely" and she was seventy-eight years old at the time! Love is truly a splendid thing, to paraphrase the famous song.

Throughout those years between 1997 and 2016, after my surgery, we managed to continue with our lovemaking on a regular basis. Although we were both in our advancing years of the sixty to seventy-year-olds, it still seemed quite natural for us. The frequency dropped but remained at a steady two or three times each week.

Our methods changed slightly as we adapted to the constraints of old age and the physical changes in my body after the cancer. It was still very pleasurable and still a necessary physical expression of our love for each other. We both achieved orgasms every time we made love up until 2016, the year of Val's stroke.

Earlier in this chapter, I mentioned that Val graduated from being pupil to being mistress in her sexual skills over our long marriage. That was so true. If she wanted me to pay particular attention to a specific part of her body, or to make love to her in a particular way, adopt a certain position or to increase the intensity or to slow it down, she would not hesitate to tell me and to insist that I conform. She would always want me to take the lead, or appear to be doing so! I recall with some fondness two particular things that she initiated on more than one occasion in the bedroom.

Firstly, we were well into the throes of our lovemaking when she suddenly pulled my head close to her and began whispering in my ear. To my amazement, for the first time in our life together, she began using rather coarse and vulgar expressions for what she wanted from me. She used a vocabulary that was unheard of from her, and it was quite a shock to me. Later, all was explained when she told me that she had read that some men liked it during the sex act, so she thought she would see if it turned me on. It didn't, as it happened. I knew that such language was completely alien to Val, and it had the opposite rather than the intended effect on me.

The second occasion that comes to mind happened later in our lives, well after my cancer surgery. We were well into our late seventies, in fact. One night, we were preparing to get ready for bed as usual. I wondered where Val had got to, as I was already in bed and she was nowhere to be seen; still in the bathroom, I assumed. Then it happened. A hand suddenly switched off the main bedroom lights, leaving only dim bedside lights in the room. Suddenly Val appeared at the end of the bed wearing the most exquisite lingerie I had ever seen in my life. She had secretly bought the underwear – bra, briefs and some sort of negligee – and she was giving me a fashion show in private, simply to excite me. For a seventy-plus-year-old woman, she looked great to me, still petite, under eight stone and just over five foot tall, hair loose over her shoulders; sure I was excited! Although we both ended up in fits of laughter, as I slowly played the game and took off the flimsy undies, it was one of many memorable nights we had in bed. A postscript to the above is that I have recently come across 'that' lingerie by Charnos, discreetly hidden in Val's underwear drawer of her wardrobe.

That my darling wife should have tried so hard to please me, even in old age, in the bedroom is quite remarkable and yet further testament to the love that we had for each other over sixty-one years of marriage.

After two years in the care home, by November 2018, Val's dementia was taking its toll. There were signs that the illness was creeping up on her. I was always aware of this and I tried to monitor it and make my behaviour towards her as appropriate as I could. My prime concern every day, for those precious moments we were together, was to ease her suffering and try to make her as happy as I was able to. Whenever the opportunity came we would make for the sun lounge, where we would sit together on the sofa and be alone. Val would only do this if the sun lounge was empty. If other residents or visitors got there before us, she declined my invitation. After a while, we became quite adept at choosing the best times. We would settle on the comfortable furniture and I would slip my arms around her thin shoulders, pulling her against me, holding her hand in my own. Sometimes we would chat. She would talk about the lovely view to Shaldon or about her family or some distant memory that had slipped back into her brain. Often, after a very short period of time, Val would cuddle up against me, put her head on my chest and slip into sleep. It was quite wonderful. We would stay there for an hour or more like that. Occasionally, she would adjust her own position and hold me more tightly. She adored me and her body sent that clear message during those times. She felt safe, she held me and I was still her rock. I did manage to keep her close and my arms around her, although at times I was myself in great discomfort and even pain from the position I was in. Thinking back now, I am so very grateful for those hours, over many days, that the Almighty gave us together, a bonus at the end of our many happy years of marriage. Lots of the care staff coming and going would comment about seeing us there, with much delight.

One day in November 2018 we were in the sun lounge, cuddled up together, when I was aware that Val's hands were on the move. She seemed to be asleep, possibly dreaming. I was amazed to find that her hand had moved down to my thigh and that she was gently caressing me! It must have lasted only a few minutes but it was clear that she was caressing me in an openly sexual manner. She was enjoying it. Whatever semi-conscious state she was in, I'll never know, but her intentions were quite clear. Of course, it was something she had done many times, thousands of times throughout our marriage. Here she was, eighty-two years old, her body wracked with end-of-life syndrome aches and pains, her mind distorted with the onset of vascular dementia, and, albeit for a few minutes, she was virtually making love to me! What a testimony to our love of more than sixty-three years!

I mentioned earlier in this chapter that Val was constantly amazed by what she learned from her female friends about their sexual experiences. Throughout our own long and happy marriage, we often discussed this and we were both appalled and upset about it. It was clear that many husbands didn't understand, couldn't be bothered, or simply didn't care about their wives' needs in bed. It was as if all that mattered was that the husband, the man, was satisfied; good sex was for men. Sadly, this old-fashioned Victorian view is still around today. Many wives, who love their husbands dearly, still do not experience the wonderful sex life that it is possible for them to achieve. Val and I had a superb physical relationship over many years. As I have said before, that was to a great extent because of the deep love we had for each other. It was also the result of our belief that we should both give each other the most pleasure we could possibly give and of knowing how to do that.

In the early years of our marriage, we discussed our own sex life quite often, usually when we were in bed. There were important things that we needed to know about each other and we had to discuss them openly and honestly. Luckily, we had similar views and thoughts on these things and this, because of our mutual understanding and love, meant that we had a consensus which lasted all through our marriage. Both of us had no interest in pornography, sadism, masochism or indeed homosexuality. '*Fifty Shades of Grey*' were not for us! In fact, you could say that we both considered such things as perversions of true lovemaking. Rightly or wrongly, it was what we felt and stood by; such things were anathema to both of us and we didn't change our views over sixty-one years together.

My aim was always to make Val happy in every aspect of life after her sad early childhood. Through travel, through loving her so much and through the physical side of our marriage, we achieved much together. Val experienced the wonders of multiple orgasms all through our marriage and I was always satisfied too, not least in the knowledge that I had been responsible for her pleasure and she for mine.

I am pleased to say in concluding this chapter that in these final years of my own life I can still remember in great detail making love to my darling Val, from frequent and quite fantastic nights and days in Singapore, enhanced by the exotic environment and the tropical heat, through many years to our late seventies when Val could still say to me after our lovemaking, "That was lovely," and mean it. I still today look at photographs of her and DVD movies of her when she was much younger and I feel a warm glow, and not a little excitement.

Chapter 11

The Final Years

The previous chapter, *In the Bedroom*, was difficult for me to write. This final chapter is equally challenging but for quite different reasons. I had long thought that I would write this final chapter in a straightforward way, simply documenting the events as they happened chronologically. Inevitably, I would find myself writing with some emotion on the events. This would, however, bring what I feel would be an inappropriate and unwelcome amount of sadness to the book in general. It would diminish and undermine what is in reality a very happy story. A true story of great love written from the heart and, indeed, soul. I have now decided, therefore, not to make this final chapter a sad end to a wonderful journey but rather an inspirational and hope-filled end to the journey that Val and I took together over sixty-three years.

There is another reason for this change of heart on my part. After Val's death in February 2019, devastated,

I embarked on the sad journey through my bereavement and personal grief. I wrote about this journey, as it happened to me, in a small book which was published in 2020, entitled *Love Never Ends*. Having written about Val's final days and her passing, when it was still affecting me so greatly in emotional terms, I feel that should be enough of sadness.

During the years leading up to 2015 we settled into a very pleasant life together. To be honest, all our years together had been quite wonderful, as I hope the reader will have gathered from previous chapters. We were happy living in Dawlish; our bungalow was small in comparison to our previous house in Exeter. It was enough for us with the added bonus of a large rear garden which Val really adored. It contained a large mature apple tree which gave us an ample supply of delicious Bramley apples each year. Val would enjoy cooking an excellent variety of apple dishes, from the humble blackberry and apple tart to crumbles and often some quite exotic fare! She would supply our grateful neighbours with bags of apples each year on a regular basis. She also loved tending the flower borders and the flowering bushes too. We spent many delightful hours in the spring and summer simply sitting together on the patio or further down the garden, reading or just sunbathing and talking. We had over the years enhanced the rear garden with the addition of a summer house, tool shed and eventually 'Val's own hut', which I managed to build for her when well into my late seventies! That had come about because I had taken over the summer house in pursuit of my hobby of more than fifty years: amateur radio. Val happily allowed me to create my radio shack in the summer house and she never complained when I would vanish for an hour or so into my 'shack', communicating with the rest of the world. It was the practical application of our long-agreed decision that we would always have time to ourselves without hindrance or argument. Neither of us would ever abuse this. We simply accepted it; Val would play her piano, read or listen to music and I would be tuning the airwaves, gathering news and information from around the world.

The space and the time that we had to do our own thing proved invaluable, and I am convinced that it strengthened our marriage over so many years. I can picture vivid scenes even now of Val coming down the garden path with a tray; hot drinks with biscuits or homemade cakes. She would tap on the door of the summer house and join me for an informal small meal. This would happen during the day or late at night. I would reciprocate by preparing refreshments on occasion, quietly putting them down for her beside the piano, sitting down in the room and enjoying her music, without disturbing her at all.

We did not do this every day, of course. Alongside these 'times apart' but in the same bungalow, we spent hours together in our lounge, reading, watching TV or a DVD film. We enjoyed our lives together so much. We frequently went out for walks. The close proximity of the seashore, merely four minutes away, was an added bonus. We would walk to Dawlish Warren via the coastal cliffs, enjoying a lunch out at a clifftop hotel. We were blessed to be able to see the sea from both front and rear gardens of the bungalow.

Punctuating this lovely lifestyle would be many holidays. We still visited Cornwall, where we had a caravan, and made one trip per year to Scotland. We did drastically cut down on our overseas trips as we got older, but we did manage to visit Austria on two or three occasions in the final years. I remember visiting Igls, just outside Innsbruck, where I witnessed Val swimming several lengths of our hotel's swimming pool with some delight. We also had two weeks in an apartment at St Gilgen in the Tyrolean Lake District when we were well into our seventies!

Val continued to attend Cofton WI meetings once a month and she maintained her local friendships with neighbours. She was also a regular member of the church congregation at St Gregory's in Dawlish, where I also attended, on the odd occasion only, I must sadly admit.

I am so glad that I was able to fulfil yet another of Val's dreams, near the end of her life: our visit to the Anne Frank House, in Amsterdam. I recently looked at Val's well-thumbed copy of *The Diary of Anne Frank* on our bookshelves here in the bungalow. It brought it all back to me. It was the year 2015 and at the age of seventy-nine we were wondering if we should even attempt another foreign holiday. We were daunted by the thought of airports and all the hassle of overseas travel at our age. The attractions of our well-loved St Buryan in Cornwall, where we had a luxury caravan by then, or even a trip to Scotland, seemed the most likely outcome. Talking about it one evening, I asked Val if there was still anywhere in Europe that she had always wanted to go. She thought about it for a while and then she mentioned Anne Frank's house. I didn't comment at the time but I thought about it secretly for days and days. I am now so glad that I made the decision. I kept it a secret from Val until I had made the necessary search for the possibilities that were available; eventually, I made the arrangements. We would fly to Amsterdam from Exeter Airport and spend four days in a modest hotel there. Val was really delighted.

We managed to overcome all the usual problems, such as struggling with cases on Schiphol Airport's escalators, the packed train into Amsterdam and finding our hotel. We really felt our age on arrival when we settled down for our first night in the hotel; we were exhausted. The next day, we discovered to our horror that there were very large queues around Anne Frank's house; it seemed that all the world's travellers had descended on Amsterdam at the same time and that they all wanted to see Anne Frank's house. It was almost impossible to contemplate us ever being able to visit the place. Val was so disappointed and close to tears. We had given up on the idea by the evening and we decided to drown our sorrows with a few drinks in our hotel's bar. Val eventually went up to our room, leaving me to finish a whisky at the bar. I began a conversation with the hotel's manager and explained to him what had happened and just how disappointed we were. I was delighted when he offered to help. It seems that there were ways to overcome the problem of having to queue in order to gain entry to the '*Huis*' as he called it. I slipped him a rather large Euro banknote and he said he would see what he could do!

Full of hope rather than expectation, I found the manager early the next morning; I had not mentioned any of this to Val. The manager smiled at me and handed me an envelope. Inside were two priority tickets and booking confirmation to visit Anne Frank's house at 11 am that day; we did not have to join the enormous queue. It would have been impossible for us to stand in a queue like that for most of the day anyway. I excitedly went off to show Val what I had managed to achieve. It all went well. We took a taxi from the hotel to the '*Huis*' and walked past the huge queue straight into the building. I must confess, however, that we only managed to climb the many stairs to the top rooms with considerable difficulty. We were exhausted when we arrived back at our hotel for lunch. The hugs and kisses that Valerie gave me and her obvious delight and happiness made it a wonderful day to remember. That proved to be the last holiday we ever had together abroad, and it will always remain a very special memory for me. Four years later, my dear Val passed away after several years of illness and suffering.

Things started to change for us as the year 2016 unfolded. Val had been blessed with good health throughout her adult life. She had never been an inpatient in any hospital before she was eighty years old! She only ever suffered the occasional winter cold or cough, nothing serious. In 2016, all this changed, for her and for us. She suffered a stroke early that year. This was not immediately evident, and it was only discovered later that year when she began to behave oddly. Investigations, including brain scans, revealed the stroke and brain damage. Unusually, the stroke did not cause her any speech problems or affect her mobility. It did, however, bring about the onset of vascular dementia.

After fifty-eight years of a very happy marriage and life together, this came as a devastating shock to me. Quite naturally, I had expected us to continue to grow old together, adapting our life as the years went by. Who could anticipate, or even contemplate, this happening? Why was it happening? This wonderful caring woman, who had suffered in her childhood, was suffering again. In those desperate first few days after her diagnosis, I prayed as I have never prayed before. Please allow us to have some more time together. You have given us a wonderful fifty-eight years of happiness; please give us a little more time.

My prayers were answered almost immediately. It was the first of many miracles. Miracle is the only suitable word to explain the next two years of our life together. Although there were some difficult times, we were blessed with a 'bonus' two years of happiness together. I prayed daily that Val's dementia would not stop her recognising me and knowing me. I dreaded the thought of that happening.

After more than six weeks in the specialist psychiatric assessment unit of a hospital, suitably medicated, she returned to me, at home. As per the prognosis, she deteriorated so much that I could not care for her at home, even with adequate support. Val had to go into a specialist residential care home. I visited her every day, spending four or five hours with her. We had lunch together in her room. We talked, we held hands, we listened to music, we went for walks outside the care home and we even had cuddles in the sun lounge! Val knew me all the time.

She would often be waiting for me to arrive, sitting patiently near the front door of the home. She would be delighted to see me; she welcomed my kiss of greeting and hug, and we would go off to her room. I would spend more and more time with her as the months went by, including in the later months sitting in a chair beside her bed at night. Whenever I was with her she knew me, and I thank God for that. We had a noticeboard full of photos facing her bed. The photos were mainly from our travels. I remember just a few days before she died, she suddenly sat up in bed, pointed to a photo of our wedding day and said, "That's our wedding day!" Val loved music and literature. She played the piano and she worked as a bookseller for many years. Sadly, the dementia stopped her reading for herself, but the love of music remained with her to the end. I would play her favourite CDs in her room and she would sing and hum to them. When there were no CDs on, she would insist on listening to Classic FM on the radio. She would often tell me off for not naming a symphony or composer correctly! The music was a great comfort to her, but it was so sad to see her deteriorate over the months.

Her frustration was always present. "I don't know what to do or say," was a frequent comment from her. The indignity and distress caused by her many physical problems, such as incontinence, added to the pain for both of us. She was still my wonderful wife, however, and God gave us that to the end. After spending many hours with her, I would often telephone her late in the evenings. Sometimes she wouldn't want to speak to me, but the carers were good; they judged the situation accordingly and would make plausible excuses for me. Most times, Val wanted to speak to me. I remember on several occasions I phoned and the carer would go to take the mobile phone to her and I could hear my darling wife's voice. "Is that my beloved John?" she would say distinctly. Those were lovely words for me to overhear so near her end.

In just over two years, I missed visiting Val on half a dozen days. I built up a routine in order to drive to her care home each day, some six miles from our home here in Dawlish. Those few days that I did miss were the result of my illnesses, including two operations in hospital. Luckily, Val's dementia and poor memory meant that she made light of my absence and greeted me lovingly when I appeared again. The miracles that I hinted at earlier included allowing us to celebrate our Diamond Wedding anniversary in the care home, complete with cake and a party. Also two Christmas celebrations and our birthdays. Val celebrated her eighty-third birthday just twenty-six days before she died. Although she had the medical 'end-of-life syndrome' by this time and was bedridden, with morphine medication, she still managed to blow out the candles on her birthday cake; the miracles continued.

A week before she died, I was sitting by her bed holding her hand when the team leader carer came into the room with another carer. They had come to 'turn' Val, who was now bedridden. We were chatting together and somehow the subject of France came up. I told the two carers about Val's love of France and that she was a fluent French speaker. Val couldn't or didn't join in the conversation, just lying there, but awake. I added that she could even sing the French National Anthem in French, all the verses. For some reason, I began to sing the chorus of the *Marseillaise* aloud, "*Marchons, marchons ....*" On hearing this, Val amazed us all by pulling herself up in her bed and singing the next verse, in French, at the top of her voice! It was a strange but wonderful little scene to witness. The carers were flabbergasted and there was a stunned few minutes of silence as Val collapsed back down on her bed. This was just five days before she died.

On Saturday 16th February 2019, I knew my darling Val was near the end. She was no longer eating or drinking and she was following the path that her GP and the attendant district nurses had predicted. When I arrived in the morning, two district nurses were there, giving Val injections and attending to her needs. I sat holding her hand, but she was unconscious most of the time. After a few hours and many cups of tea, I asked the nurses if I should stay. They didn't think it would happen that day, so eventually I left and drove home.

In the afternoon, I was at home listening to a football match on my radio. A keen football fan, nothing would stop me from doing that! At about four o'clock something made me switch off the radio and a voice in my head told me to phone the care home. I am now convinced that the Almighty had spoken to me at the time! I telephoned the care home and was told that Val had deteriorated and that they were glad that I had phoned. I rushed into the care home, where I found Val struggling with 'death-rattle' breathing.

I sat by her bed, holding her left hand in my own. We remained like this for many hours. At ten o'clock, something, I believe now it was God, told me to move closer to Val. I still held her left hand closely in my own. I moved up from my chair and sat on the edge of the bed, putting my right arm around her thin shoulders and pulling her against me. Something or someone told me to say, "The Almighty is waiting for you, my darling." Immediately, Val's right hand came across and covered my left hand so that she was holding my hand in both of hers. Her eyes opened and she looked at me directly. Her two hands squeezed mine; the deathly rattle of her breathing stopped and she was gone to her maker. I kissed her still warm head and told her that I loved her. She had died in my arms, holding my hand, knowing I was there, in a very wonderful and special way. I could not have asked for a better ending, and I do thank Almighty God for all His blessings on that day.

Epilogue

Throughout our life together, Val and I were blessed with some of the things that help make a good marriage. We had a mutual understanding between us and a deep love; we respected each other. These things combined to make it easier to face up to and overcome both minor and major difficulties that we faced over the years. When there were sad times we accepted them together, and the happy times were much more enjoyable because we shared them. Our marriage was an equal partnership sustained by our love. Over many years, it became something that, in a quite wonderful way, got stronger as we grew older.

When Val died on the 16th of February 2019, every aspect of our shared life was gone forever. The jokes we laughed at, our memories, the music, meals and time together, plans we made. I am still aware of the physical reminders today; the unslept-on side of the bed, her clothes, the touch of her hand, her being there for me, doing everything with me. We shared so much as a couple for a long, long time.

This book has been an attempt to remind myself and others of some of our happy life together. Remembrance is so important for those of us who are still here. I feel privileged that I am able to provide a record, however limited and inadequate, of our sixty-one years of marriage. Very happy years and a true love story.